WEIRD SHORT STORIES

WRITTEN BY

MARK D. BRADLEY

ISBN: 1-4033-3655-5 (Electronic)
ISBN: 1-4033-3656-3 (Softcover)

This book is printed on acid free paper.

1stBooks – rev. 06/14/02

This book is dedicated to Megan Ware

Special Thanks to: Helen L. and Oceanus Bradley

My brothers and sisters

Debra A. Harris

Sheila Ware

Wanda and Stephanie Dean

All future and past associates

Mark D. Bradley is from Lincoln Heights, Ohio, a suburb north of Cincinnati. He has written numerous un-published poems, short stories, and songs. This book is the first of many books and novels that he will be publishing in the near future. Mark D. Bradley is very well traveled and is very well educated. The stories that he writes are related to some of his life experiences. Using a very vivid imagination, he writes stories that you want to read over and over again. His laid back approach to life and to writing makes his work very understandable and very easy to read.

CONTENTS

INTRODUCTION ix

1. WEIRD SHORTS 1

2. LOVELY FLOWERS 7

3. MY COOKIES.. 15

4. BIRD 23

5. RAISING MY ASIA 31

6. OLD PEOPLE... 38

7. OUT OF BODY 43

8. TELEPHONE LOVE 48

9. I, MURDERER 53

10. CASANOVA BROWN.. 57

11. BUBBLE CHILD.. 63

12. MANSTERS 70

13. CLOWNS.. 75

14. RESTRAINING ORDER 80

15. GIRL TALK... 85

16. DADDY 92

17. GREEN...98

18. LOVE LETTER TO MY BOO 103

19. FARMER IN THE DELL 106

20. STOP SIGN..115

21. FIEND 119

22. LITTLE GIRL LOST 126

23. WORKING WITH DEATH.......................................132

ABOUT THE AUTHOR...137

INTRODUCTION

By Mark D. Bradley

"WEIRD SHORT STORIES", is a collection of fictional stories that describe many different scenarios that happen or could happen to people. These stories are about the not so normal things. Some of the stories explore the mysteries of life, possibly the supernatural. There are stories about the crazy things that people do. Some of the stories are simply tales of very odd coincidences. Stories of love, in it's many forms, are also included. All of the stories are a little strange and a little weird. These strange and weird stories come together to form a very entertaining book of short stories. I hope that you enjoy reading them as much as I enjoyed writing them.

Mark D. Bradley

1. WEIRD SHORTS

The answer to how my grandfather became a wealthy man, has always been a mystery to me. Wealth can make some people act very strange. My grandfather was very strange indeed. In the last couple of years of his life, he became very introverted and lived in isolation. Grandfather was not as strange as Howard Hughes but he was getting there. Nobody had even seen or heard from my grandfather in over a year. When grandfather died, I was his only living relative. I inherited everything that grandfather owned. Money, cars, clothes, jewels, property, everything was mine. I had always been a very unlucky person. After two divorces, bankruptcy, and more of my share of jail time, finally, Lady Luck had smiled upon me.

Grandfather's house was huge. It was much bigger than I could have ever imagined it to be. The house was very clean. Some would say that the house was in showroom condition. I had to sit down for awhile in order to take it all in. Grandfather had style and a taste for the elegant. Me, myself, I have never had any style. For the last six months, I had been living in a rat and roach infested room on the shady side of town. Needless to say, this was quite a step up for me. Keeping this big house in good shape was going to be much too much for a simple guy like me to do. I had never been a homeowner nor did I ever plan to be. My plan was to live in grandfather's house until I could sell it. Then I would buy me a a condo in the suburbs.

After the I.R.S. took the money that was due them, I was left with about ten million dollars to spend any way I wanted to. First I had to go out and hire me some professional investors and consultants. I bought my fair share of toys and trinkets but I was also very conservative with my spending. Surprisingly, I did not go on any wild shopping sprees. I made sure that I took my time while making monetary decisions. Ending up broke again was not going to happen to me.

Eventually, I had to go thru my grandfather's belongings. The things that I liked, I kept. The things that I did not like, I gave them away or trashed. My grandfather had style and elegance when it came to houses, furniture, and cars, but his taste in clothing was very bad. I donated all of grandfather's clothing to the Salvation Army. It took two trucks to haul away all of those horrible clothes. I filled all of my closets and dresser drawers with designer clothing. Now that I was rich, I had to dress the part. While putting away some of my brand new designer underwear, I found an ugly pair of my grandfather's Bermuda shorts. I thought that I had gotten rid of all of grandfather's clothes. I don't know how I missed those weird shorts, but obviously I did. The next day, I took those weird shorts and a few other items to the Salvation Army drop off center. Later that afternoon, after working out at the gym, I took a long and refreshing shower. I opened one of my dresser drawers to get some clean underwear and to my surprise, those weird shorts were neatly folded on top of my new designer underwear. I was perplexed. In a frenzied state, I grabbed those weird shorts, drove to the the city garbage dump, and tossed those weird shorts on top of a garbage pile. I was somewhat relieved as I drove home, but I had to be sure. I proceeded up the stairs, very cautiously, to the Master Bedroom. I opened my dresser drawer and there they were, folded neatly on top of my brand new designer underwear. I started cussing and talking to myself. Was this some kind of cruel joke being being played on me? Was I losing my sanity just when things were getting better for me? I came to my senses. I grabbed a match and started a red hot fire in my fireplace. I grabbed those cursed weird shorts and threw them in the fire. I watched as those weird shorts burned and became ashes. I checked my dresser drawer to see if those weird shorts would reappear. They did not. Finally the nightmare was over. Those weird shorts were out of my house and destroyed. I fell into a sound and relaxing sleep. When I woke up the next day, I was horrified. Those weird shorts were wrapped around my left hand. I had never been so scared in my life, and I do not scare very easily, but the sight of those shorts made me poo poo on myself. I threw those weird shorts off my hand and fled the house. I drove off in my car smelling rather foul. I checked into the first motel that I came across. I showered and cried. I ordered some comfort food and I ordered some clothes delivered to my room. I tried to sleep my trouble away. I tossed and turned all night. I woke up screaming. I was now wearing those weird shorts. I tried desperately to get those weird shorts off of me. I tried ripping them off but they would not rip. I tried cutting them off but they would not cut. I pulled and I tugged. I tugged and I pulled. They were not coming off. I decided to wear a pair of pants over those weird shorts. The pants fell off of me and turned into dust. I was very unhappy, disgusted, and embarrassed. I did not want to be seen with those weird shorts on. I waited until nightfall. When it was pitch black outside, assured that the coast was clear, I ran to my car. I drove around awhile in a funk. Finally, I decided to drive back home. I entered my house and went into the living room. I sat down in the middle of the living room floor and just stared into the fireplace. Eventually, I fell to sleep.

I woke up the next day feeling like a completely different person. My fear was gone. I was in a very good mood. Those weird shorts that I was wearing no longer looked weird. As a matter of fact, I liked the way that they looked on me. I no longer wanted to take them off or get rid of them. Crazy right? No I was quite sane. I felt extremely confident, confident enough to walk into town. I walked the whole five miles, never breaking a sweat. On the way to town, several people, including some very pretty ladies, offered to ride me into town. I declined their offers and kept on walking. I had never been offered rides before, especially from pretty ladies. When I arrived in town, I stopped in a store to buy a bottle of water. I bought a bottle of water and, for some reason, I bought a lottery ticket. To my astonishment, I won one million dollars on an instant win ticket. Suddenly, the light bulb in my head came on. I understood completely. Those weird shorts were the source of grandfather's wealth. Not only did those weird shorts make you wealthy, they also made you wise and confident. Those weird shorts changed my grandfather and now they were changing me.

It has been nearly fifty years since I found out about my grandfather's secret. I have amassed quite a fortune. I married a beautiful lady who stayed faithfully by my side until her death a few short months ago. I had a son who made me a proud grandfather. I have become a world renowned gift giver to the less fortunate people of the world. It's been a wonderful life. Unfortunately, nobody lives forever. Even the power of those weird shorts can't stop death from coming. When I die, my grandson will inherit all that I own, including those weird shorts. He will find them or they will find him. Will he understand? WEIRD SHORTS have a way of making you understand.

2. LOVELY FLOWERS

The silence of the early morning is interrupted by the crowing of a rooster perched on a white picket fence. The crowing can be heard for many miles. The crowing is both soothing and eerie at the same time. This is a wake up call for all of mankind. The hypnotic beauty of the rising sun is overshadowed by the brilliant, vibrant colors of the Lovely Flowers. Every morning, brings with it, a brand new day. Each new day is filled with promise. No day should ever be wasted or taken for granted. Wise men have told us, over and over again, that tomorrow is not promised to us. We must live each day to it's fullest splendor. We soon realize that time waits for no one.

Linda Ellen Smith, known by townfolk as the Chicken Lady, has a chicken farm. The farm is five miles east of the rural town called Shonuff. Her chickens are always the biggest and always the best that money can buy. She is always winning blue ribbons and prizes at the local fairs. Each year, the number of chickens on her farm increases while the number of people living in the area decreases. Linda Ellen

Smith is an elderly lady, a senior citizen. She is well over one hundred years old. She is very nice, probably the sweetest person around. Folks say that she is a little too sweet and too much sugar is not good for you. The rumor mill says that she has a son but he is never seen and there is no birth certificate or any other documentation verifying his birth. There is a very strange looking scarecrow in Linda Ellen Smith's cornfield. It is always in different positions and always dressed in different outfits. The scarecrow seems to be moving around on it's own. Some folks say that if you get a close look at the scarecrow, you would swear that it was alive.

Charlie Wilson and his family are passing through town on their way to the big city. They are looking for a place to stay for the night. Mr. Charlie Wilson has his wife and three kids with him. His wife, Velvet, is a former fashion model. She is extremely vain, has a huge ego, and is quite a bitch most of the time. His only son, Junior, is bad to the bone. Relatives swear that Junior is either retarded or possessed. Last but not least are Charlie's adopted twin girls, Megan and Lyncoyia. The twins are very nice kids and seem out of place as members of Charlie Wilson's family. Today, in the town of Shonuff, a whole new experience awaits the Wilson family.

While driving through the town of Shonuff, Charlie spots a man walking in the street. He rolls down his window and questions the man. charlie: Excuse me sir. My family and I have traveled a very long way and we are very tired. Is there somewhere in town that provides lodging, a hotel or motel? MAN: We don't have any hotels or motels here, but there are plenty of abandoned houses. As you can see, this is pretty much a ghost town. It seems that people pack up and leave in the middle of the night. If you need a place to stay, a real comfortable place with good eats, I suggest that you go to the Chicken Lady's house. It's a short drive south. You can't miss it. There are flowers all over the place, Lovely Flowers.

charlie: I guess that's where we will go. Thank you very much mister. (Charlie and his family drive on.)

Charlie finds the Chicken Lady's house. There are lovely, beautiful, flowers everywhere. Charlie pulls in her driveway and parks. An elderly, smiling lady comes out of the house. She has a large pitcher of ice cold lemonade and some drinking cups. Charlie greets her.

charlie: Good morning miss. I was told by a man in town, that my family might might be able to stay here for the night. We are tired and weary from traveling. If you have any rooms to rent, we would like to rent them.

chicken lady: This is your lucky day sonny. The house is empty and a very lonely place right now. It has been quite a while since I have had any guest. Come on inside out of the heat and have yourselves some ice cold lemonade. My name is Linda Ellen Smith, but you can call me Grandma Ellen. Some people call me the Chicken Lady, but I don't mind. Make sure that you walk on the sidewalk and try not to step on the flowers. My son and I really love our flowers.

velvet: I have never seen so many beautiful flowers. They are truly lovely. You and your son are superb gardeners.

chicken lady: We try to keep them well watered and well fed. You can call it a labor of love. That's enough about flowers, come on inside and look the place over. (Everybody goes inside except Junior.

He lags behind and stomps on some of the flowers. The flowers scream out loud in pain. A frightened Junior runs inside the house.)

megan: You have a really big house Grandma Ellen. Why are your walls covered with pictures of chickens? Why are the chickens dressed up in clothes? You must really love chickens.

chicken lady: So many questions. So many questions. Yes, I do love my chickens. They are like family to me. People say that I have chicken in my blood. Let me show you to your rooms, then I will eat you for lunch.

junior: What did you say old lady?

chicken lady: I said that I will heat you some lunch. You all must be awful hungry. Let's see if Grandma Ellen can fatten you up a bit before night falls. First I am going to tend to my chil... chickens. You all can freshen up and get ready for a delicious meal. (After getting cleaned up, the Wilson's enter the dining room. On the dining room table is a meal fit for a king. The Chicken Lady enters the dining room.) chicken lady: I hope that you don't mind if the twins eat with me outside. I have something a little different prepared for them.

charlie: We don't mind at all Grandma Ellen. They are well behaved and you won't have any problems with them. Now Junior is another story. He has to stay here with me so that I can watch him. (Grandma Ellen and the twins go outside and sit at a picnic table. Sitting on the picnic table, are three bowls of corn. Meanwhile, back inside of the house, Charlie, Velvet, and Junior are gorging themselves.) chicken lady: I hope that they eat enough. I don't want to have to make any more potion. (Day has become night. Linda Ellen Smith and the twins enter the dining room.)

chicken lady: I hope that you all had enough to eat. If you are finished, you can go to your rooms and relax. The twins and I will clear the table and do the dishes.

junior: I don't want to go to my room. It smells like a dead cat in there. Can I sleep in the car?

charlie: You can sleep with my foot in your behind if you don't behave. Excuse my language Grandma Ellen.

chicken lady: There is no need to excuse yourself Charlie. The little monster, I mean, the little youngster can sleep in my son's room. It always smells like fresh flowers in that room. There is a nice big bed and a lovely view of the flower garden. (At midnight, the twins are awakened by Grandma Ellen. They hold each other in a loving embrace. They go outside and walk to a small henhouse.)

chicken lady: Welcome home my children. You have gathered a nice trio of fresh flowers for our dying planet. Our little adoption plan worked out rather nicely. (Grandma Ellen and the twins are changing, changing into chickens. The small henhouse is glowing. Grandma Ellen and the twins vanish inside of the henhouse. A long line of chickens has formed at the henhouse. The chickens enter one by one, vanishing inside of the henhouse. The henhouse transforms into a pyramid. The midnight sky turns bright red as the pyramid rises into deep space. Thunder and lightning fills the sky. Something is coming to town and it's not Santa Claus.) All of the flowers around the house began chanting, "We want Junior". Junior wakes up startled and afraid. The loud chants from the flowers is hurting his ears. His body feels like it is on fire. He tries to scream but he can't. Junior is changing, changing into a burning bush. The Chicken Lady's son, the man Charlie Wilson talked to in town, the scarecrow from the cornfield, is standing in the doorway. He has a big flower pot in his hands and a big grin on his face. He picks up the burning bush plant, plants it inside the flower pot, and puts the potted bush neatly on the front porch.

Charlie and Velvet Wilson wake up suddenly from their sleep. The flowers are singing. The Wilsons look at each other and begin to scream in terror. They are changing into flowers. Their nice comfortable bed changes into a flower bed. They are outside, planted with the rest of the flowers.

Gone are the people of Shonuff. Gone are their imaginations and their dreams. Greed and selfishness made them blind to the mysterious things around them. All that I see, as I watch from my cornfield, are Lovely Flowers.

3. MY COOKIES

Long, long ago, before Amos was famous, I made My Cookies. In my opinion, they were the best cookies ever made. In a little town, in a little bakery, in a big kitchen, I made My Cookies. They were so delicious. They melted inside your mouth. My Cookies were the crunchiest cookies around, thanks to my secret ingredient. Unlike the big cookie companies, I used all natural ingredients. I used home grown, from my own little farm, ingredients. The ingredient that made my cookies special, was my organic flour. My flour gave the cookies their texture and crunch. I did not give my cookies a catchy name. They did not need a catchy name. They stood out on their own. They were simply known as My Cookies. That is what people asked for when they placed an order, My Cookies.

I got the recipe for My Cookies from my grandmother. I had just turned twelve years old. My parents and I were living in an apartment in Chicago. It was springtime and my father's mother was visiting us. She had made the long trip from Jackson, Mississippi. It was her first and only visit. She did not like it up North. Grandmother was very old but she still knew her way around the kitchen. She could really cook!! I woke up one morning to the smell of fresh baked cookies. There is, in my opinion, nothing in the world better to wake up to. My grandmother was not in the best of health. She had high blood pressure and was a diabetic. She was suppose to leave the sweets alone. I guess her sweet tooth was just too powerful to overcome because she was always cooking something sweet. Grandma saw the hungry puppy dog look on my face. She asked me if I wanted some cookies. She did not have to ask me twice. I poured myself a glass of milk and I began to pig out on those cookies. Those cookies were great. They tasted oh so good. Immediately, I was addicted to them. They had a crunch to them that I had never experienced before. I was a cookie expert and to me, these were the best. They were really special. My mother came home from work that evening and smelled the fresh baked cookies. The aroma had traveled all over the apartment. Some of our neighbors were in the hallway trying to get a smell contact. My mother asked me who had baked cookies. I told her that grandmother had baked the cookies. I told her that they were the best cookies in the world. My mother told me that we had run out of flour the day before. She asked where had grandmother gotten flour so early in the morning. I told my mother that my grandmother must have borrowed the flour from our neighbors. Later, It came to me. Grandmother had never left the apartment that day. I asked grandmother how did she bake cookies when we did not have any flour. Grandmother told me that she had made her own flour.

Cockroaches are not the world's favorite insect. People see them as nasty and disgusting pests. They have excellent survival skills and they multiply very fast. Chances are, if you spot one running around inside of your house, there are probably a couple of hundred more of them hiding around somewhere. While my grandmother was living with us, I did not see any cockroaches. Apparently, the cockroaches were good to bake with too. That was the source of the flour that grandmother used to bake cookies that day. Sometimes older people, on fixed income, have to be resourceful. Grandmother did not have a lot of money, but she was a very proud woman. One of my cousins told me that, when he visited grandmother, he would see a lot of dog food and cat food cans in her pantry. Grandmother did not have a dog or a cat. I asked grandmother why she made flour out of cockroaches instead of borrowing flour from the neighbors. She said her flour made better cookies. She told me that years ago, while eating her Raisin Bran cereal, she noticed that her cereal tasted different, it was a lot crunchier. She put on her glasses and found that she was not eating Raisin Bran, but regular Corn Flakes with dead cockroaches in them. Since that day, she has been baking with flour made from cockroaches. It seems strange, but I understood her logic. If you find something that works for you, stick with it. I must admit, the cookies that she made out of cockroach flour, were great. Those cookies were the best I had ever had and I wanted grandmother to teach me how to make them. It was kind of disgusting at first, grinding the cockroaches up in the food processor, but I got use to it. I learned how to make My Cookies. I did some research on cockroaches. I learned that cockroaches are considered delicious in some third world countries. They are a plentiful source of protein and nutrients. Insects are a very good food source. We consume them by the billions. While in the scouts, I learned to dig for and eat grubs. I have had chocolate covered grasshoppers before. In some of the fancier restaurants, I have eaten snails. However, deep down in my gut, I know they are not going to be willing to eat foods or cookies made out of cockroaches.

I grew up, graduated from high school, and enrolled in cooking school. I wanted to be a Master Chef. I paid for my tuition by selling My Cookies. I sold them to my neighbors and to my fellow students. My Cookies were instantly the talk of the town. People were always asking for the recipe or trying to buy the recipe to make My Cookies. I knew that most people could not deal with the reality of the recipe's true composition, flour made from roaches, so I would not give or sell anybody the recipe. The popularity of My Cookies enabled me to open up my very own bakery. I was entering and winning all kinds of bakery competitions. My blue ribbons were hanging all over the walls inside of my bakery. However, most good things usually come to an abrupt end.

Soon, cookie companies from all over the world, came calling. I held out for as long as I could but it's extremely hard to turn down the kind of money that big companies can offer you. I was made an offer that I simply could not refuse. The recipe that I sold to this particular company used regular flour, not my secret roach flour. The cookies were excellent but there was definitely a noticeable difference. The company that I sold my recipe to, noticed the difference and called me to complain. I told them that they were probably not using all natural ingredients. I sold them my farm for a whole lot of money. Time after time they tried and failed to reproduce My Cookies. Once again they came crying to me. They offered me a job working for them, making My Cookies, but I was happy with my independence so I turned them down. I gave them a counter proposal that included me coming aboard as an independent consultant. My counter offer was excepted.

Companies spend lots of money buying out smaller companies. They don't know enough about the products most of the time. They try to reproduce the success of the smaller companies but they can't. They usually miss a part or an ingredient here and there. My job was to introduce the lab technicians to a new ingredient. The major complaint about their cookies was a lack of texture and a lack of crunch. In secrecy, I taught them how to make My Cookies.

I asked the C.E.O. to call a company meeting so I could personally let the cat out of the bag. A batch of My Cookies was made and served at the company meeting. All of the employees gobbled down the cookies and begged for more. After everyone had filled their stomachs, I started the meeting. I talked about nature. I explained that nature provides us with a wide variety of edible foods. I asked how many people had ever eaten pork. Nearly everyone raised their hands. I went on to explain about all of the nasty things that pigs do and about the nasty things that pigs eat. I tried to really repulse them but they just laughed. I asked how many people had eaten snails known as escargot. Half of the people raised their hands. Everyone laughed. I felt that since everybody was in such a good mood, I would just cut to the chase. I asked how many people had ever eaten food made out of roaches. I was the only one to raise my hand. They all laughed at me. I told them that they should not be laughing and that they should all have their hands raised. There was an eerie silence but I had to keep going. I told them that the cookies that they just ate were made out of roach flour.

All hell broke loose. I barely made it out of that situation with my life. The employees, like I suspected, could not handle the secret of My Cookies. I had to leave the country for a while, until things cooled down. That took about twenty years. The company that bought the recipe to My Cookies went out of business. They paid all of their employees hush money to keep quiet about the cookie situation. I don't do anymore baking. Maybe someday, if the world can ever accept my secret recipe, I will once again bake My Cookies.

4. BIRD

I have always wanted to own a pet. When I was younger, my parents promised me that they would buy me a pet someday. Someday never came. After graduating from college and getting a really good job, I decided to buy myself a pet. I did not know exactly what kind of pet that I wanted. I know that I did not want a dog, cat, or hamster. Snakes, lizards, turtles, frogs, all reptiles were out of the question. Nothing slimy for me. I thought about getting an ant farm but that would have given me the creeps. I decided to try a bird. A friend of mine had a pet chicken. That was a little too country, too bizarre for me. I decided to try a bird of some kind. I visited most of the local pet stores but nothing caught my eye. One day, while looking in the classified ads in my newspaper, I spotted an ad selling an exotic bird. The ad claimed that the bird could speak in five different languages. The ad also stated that the bird, a parrot, was maintenance free. The price was open for negotiation. This all sounded too good to be true but I was very curious. I called the number that the ad said to call. The phone rang three times. An answering machine came on and said, in a creepy voice, "Come and get your bird. It will be waiting for you at twelve midnight, at 666 Spellbinder Lane". I did not want to go but something compelled me to go and check this out.

The house was pretty easy to find. It was the only house on the street. It reminded me of one of those haunted houses that you go to on Halloween. I pulled into the driveway and got out. I walked up some old, ready to fall apart stairs. I rang the doorbell. There was a loud gong sound, so loud that it hurt my ears. The doorbell stopped ringing and the door slowly opened. I tried to turn and run back to my vehicle but something pulled me inside of the house. In a large, dimly lit room, stood a little old lady. She was about four feet tall and had very some very long, yellow fingernails. She looked like a pale corpse to me. In a deep, scary voice, she told me to follow her. She turned slowly and glided, and I do mean glided, into the next room. This room was very well lit and furnished with some very expensive furniture. In the center of the room, hanging from the ceiling, was a golden bird cage. Inside of the cage was a large white parrot. It was a wonderful bird. I had to have it. Before I could ask the little old lady for the asking price, she shouted out a price of ten thousand dollars. I looked at her like she was crazy, and she probably was. I told her that I wanted this bird but my budget was only twelve hundred dollars. She held out her nasty little hand. I reached into my wallet and gave her twelve hundred dollars. She grabbed my hand and took me to the front door. She told me that I had to go. I told her to give me my bird and a receipt. She laughed out loud and said that she was not going to give me a receipt, the bird would be at my house when I got home. For some reason I believed her. As I was pulling out of the driveway, she shouted that all sales were final, no returns or exchanges.

It did not take me a long time to get home. I was a bit spooked so I put the peddle to the metal. I pulled into my garage and parked. I sat there for a while because I was so relieved to be home. I walked around to the front entrance. I opened the door and I almost crapped my pants. Bird was sitting on my lazyboy chair, watching porno movies. I can't explain how Bird beat me home, or how it got inside my locked home and disabled my alarm system, but it did. I closed the door and walked slowly towards Bird. Bird started talking to me.

It was not speaking little phrases or a couple of words. It talked in well thought out sentences. Bird asked me why I took so long to get home and why I did not bring any beer and pretzels. I was speechless, I was in shock, I was amazed. I started having fantasies about all of the money that I could make off of Bird. Bird kept talking to me but I just walked away into my bedroom and dozed off. I must have been pretty exhausted.

I woke up the next day thinking that I had just dreamed everything that had happened that night. I found out quickly that It was not a dream. Bird flew into my bedroom, onto my bed and walked up to my face. Bird told me that we had to go over some ownership ground rules. The rules had to be followed to the letter. A lot of major changes had to be made. I did not say a word. I just listened. The more Bird talked, the angrier I became. Bird did not seem to care. Bird told me that from now on, it would only eat shrimp washed down with white wine. In a rage, I stood up and told Bird that it would eat the same food that other parrots ate, nuts, seeds, and berries. No white wine to drink, just plain old tap water is all that Bird was getting. An angry Bird flew towards my head in full attack mode, and grazed me. I picked up a broom, ready to strike Bird, ready to rumble. Bird hid behind the bed and tried to calm me down. Bird said that we had gotten way too emotional and that we needed a time out. I told Bird that the next time it tried something like that, would be the last time. Bird flew to the doorway of the bedroom, turned around, looked at me, and began a tirade of profanities. I knew then that I had made a mistake by purchasing Bird. Bird was going to be a handful. I was running late for work so I locked Bird in the basement. I would deal with Bird when I got home from work.

When I arrived at work that morning, my boss was waiting for me in the parking garage. He looked like he was angry at me for some reason. I could not think of any reason for him to be so mad at me. He approached me in a very disrespectful way. He got up in my face and started shouting at me and making threats to me. I politely asked him to back off and to tell me what his problem was. He told me that he did not like all of the nasty things that I said to him when I called him earlier in the day. I tried to tell him that I had not called him. He said that he knew what my voice sounded like and that the voice he heard was mine. He said that my telephone number was on his caller ID also. Suddenly, I knew what had happened. Somehow Bird had called my boss. I tried to calm my boss down and to explain to him what had happened, but he was just too fired up. He would probably think that I was crazy. There was no sane way to explain to him about my Bird. I ended up knocking my boss out cold with a right-left combo to his head. Needless to say, that was the end of that job. I went to a coffee shop, bought a newspaper, and started reading the want ads.

I drove around the city, trying to clear my head, trying to figure out my next move. I decided to go home and get rid of Bird. I pulled into my driveway. To my surprise, there standing at my front door, was my fiancee. What was she doing here? She was suppose to be at work. She had a nasty little frown on her face. She had her hands on her hips. She stared right thru me and just stood there looking at me. I tried to play it off. I hoped that it was just PMS but deep down inside, I knew better. I was very reluctant to leave the safety of my vehicle. I got out of the vehicle and approached her as if everything was fine. I wanted to say, how are you doing baby, but before I could say a word she smacked the taste out of my mouth. I didn't know that she could hit that hard. I almost started to cry. I was dazed but I managed to grab her hands. I restrained her while I regained my composure. I asked her why she was going off on me and she told me that I knew. She told me that I must be crazy if I think that I can talk to her any kind of way, talking to her like she was some kind of a super freak. I explained to her that I did not call her and talk disrespectful to her. I told her about Bird. The way that she looked at me, she must have thought that I had lost my mind. I told her that, if she would just calm down and come into the house, I would prove everything to her. After she calmed down, we entered the house. My bedroom door was slightly ajar. Slowly, I opened the door. My fiancee waited outside of the door while I entered. There was Bird, sitting comfortably on my bed. Beside bird was my rolodex, my cell phone, and a huge platter of shrimp. Bird asked why was I back home so early and why was I so mad looking. Bird went on to say that it knew exactly why I was home early and angry. Bird said that if I did not get with the Bird program, things were going to get a lot worse. I asked Bird who was called and what was said to them. Bird started laughing and told me that only two people were called, my boss, and my fiancee, because I needed to be taught a lesson. I cried out, Bird!! What did you say to my fiancee? Bird told me that my fiancee's voice was sexy. Her voice made Bird feel naughty so my fiancee was told to bring a couple of her freakiest girlfriends so that a foursome could happen. Bird said that my fiancee got angry and started raising her voice and cussing. Bird told her to shut up so that somebody with good sense could talk. Bird told her that being with her was like being with a crack head, then Bird hung up on her. I told Bird that it was an evil, vile, creature. Bird told me that I should be grateful that it got rid of that skinny, flat chest, stinky feet, fake haired lady. That's when all hell broke loose. My fiancee burst into the room, reached for my Louisville Slugger, and beat Bird to death. I almost felt sorry for Bird, not!! My fiancee told me that if I ever decided to get another pet, I better get a dog, a very dumb dog.

5. RAISING MY ASIA

I am surrounded by four padded walls. I sit very quiet and very still. It's not very comfortable moving around with a straight jacket on. I am planning my next move. I have some things to do and some people to see. I've been locked up far too long. Every now and then, I ask myself, why am I here? I can find no valid reason for me to still be here. Sometimes genius is mistaken for insanity. I assure you that I am quite sane. My lawyer told me to plead insane. The jury agreed that I was not guilty because of insanity. What sane person would do the things that I had done? I can't continue to play this game. I need to be free and when I am free, they will see just how crazy I really am. They think that they are helping me by keeping me in this nut house. To tell you the truth, this nut house is making me crazy. I was never, in my opinion, insane. I was just being a protective father. Is that a bad thing? A real father will do anything to protect his child. In my expert opinion, everything that I did was justified.

Asia was and always will be, my pride and joy. I named her after the great continent called Asia. Like my Asia, the continent of Asia is very beautiful. The day that I brought Asia home, from the hospital, was a beautiful day. My wife had been rushed to the hospital. She was having problems with her pregnancy. She was in so much pain. When the doctor told me that my wife and our baby had died during labor, I went into shock. I was very distraught. Everybody tried to comfort me but I was lost. I found myself walking aimlessly down hallway after hallway. I ended up walking down a hallway, with viewing areas on both sides. It was the baby ward. At that point in time, something clicked, or snapped if you talked to my shrink. Since the hospital allowed my wife and baby to die, they should not mind if I take one of these babies. I deserved something and there were plenty of babies to choose from. I looked around until I found a baby that I liked, a baby that reminded me of my wife. I picked up a cute little baby girl and left the hospital. Hospital security is not the best security around. Almost anybody can simply waltz in and waltz out. On that day, I was anybody.

I was well prepared to raise a child. During my wife's pregnancy, I read hundreds of child rearing books. I went to baby delivering classes with my wife. I changed diapers on the dolls in class. So I took my newborn baby to my home. I filed a lawsuit against the hospital and they settled out of court. Since I no longer had to work, I had more time to raise my Asia. I had a friend who was a very successful lawyer. He owed me for saving his life when we were children. I talked him into getting me all of the legal documentation that I was going to need. Once all of the legalities were taken care of, I relocated. I moved to San Diego, close to the ocean. I settled down and concentrated on raising my Asia. She was very intelligent, just her like daddy. I spent hours upon hours teaching and nurturing Asia.

The very first of my many transgressions, took place during Asia's first grade school year. I took my Asia to school everyday and picked her up when classes were over. I remember going to pick up my Asia after school one day. Something was wrong. Asia was crying. I asked her what had happened. She told me that her teacher made her stand in the dummy corner for blurting out an answer to a question. I had taught my Asia to be an aggressive and assertive student. She was only doing what she was taught. There was no reason for that teacher to embarrass my Asia. I became very angry. This teacher had to pay for hurting my baby. I took my Asia home, fed her, and waited for her to go to sleep. For my Asia's sake, I had pretended to be calm, but inside I was raging with fury. I got my brass knuckles and I went looking for my Asia's teacher. He never saw me coming. I snuck into his garage and made some noise to get him to come out and get the medicine that I had for him. It was a very savage beating. I was very unmerciful. I was on him like white on rice. He was definitely going to need a closed casket. What had started as a simple ass whooping became a brutal murder. He would probably still be alive today if only he hadn't pleaded for mercy. He did not show my Asia any mercy.

There were quite a few more such incidents that year. It must have felt good to me, a type of high that was very addictive. The one incident that really made me go off, happened during my Asia's eighth grade school year. I had told my Asia, in great detail, all about the facts of life. I didn't pull any punches. I used all of the slang words and all of the terminologies that I knew to explain to my Asia about the facts of life. I told her about all of the nasty, filthy things that little boys like to talk about. I knew that if I armed my Asia with the truth, with the facts, that she would make wise decisions. She was just experiencing puberty and she was a fine young lady. That's why I kept a watchful fatherly eye on her. I trusted my Asia but I also knew the kind of persuasive power that a slick talking young man could have over an innocent young girl. Especially when hormones are in high gear. I arrived home early one Saturday and found my Asia sitting on some boy's lap. They were kissing like grown people. I startled them when I cut on the lights. The boy took off running. I swung at him but I missed, and he got away. In a calm manner, I asked my Asia what was going on. She was crying as she told me what had happened. The young man, Jimmy Wilson, had come over to help my Asia with her homework. He sweet talked my Asia into doing a lot more than homework. I calmed my Asia down and reassured her that it was not her fault. I could never punish my Asia but that sex starved boy had to pay the price. I knew exactly what had to be done and how to do it.

On a very gloomy, rainy night, I went looking for the Wilson house. It took me a while but I found it. I peeked through the dining room window. Jimmy and his parents were having dinner. I hope that it was good because it was their last meal. I cut the phone line then I cut the power. Jimmy's father was the first to feel my wrath. I had snuck into their basement through a window. I waited for Jimmy's father to come down the stairs. He never made it to the fuse box. I made sure of that. I went up the stairs quietly. It was over quickly. I took Jimmy's family jewels as a souvenir. The next day, their maid found them and called the police. There were no clues and no motive.

There were a lot more killings. I felt completely justified because, after all, I was simply protecting my Asia. There was Asia's college sweetheart; he won't be cheating on daddy's little girl anymore. He put up a pretty good fight, but it wasn't good enough. Asia's first boss kept passing her up for promotions. He even had the nerve to cheat my Asia out of her raise. That was a bad move, a bad move indeed. Asia's first husband was abusing her. I guess he thought that he had married a punching bag. Me and my brass knuckles showed him what a real punching bag felt like.

I kept a detailed journal. That was my downfall. My nosey house keeper was cleaning my den. She found my opened journal sitting on my desk. She read some of it. She read all about my dirty deeds. Instead of turning me in to the police, she tried to black mail me. She wanted to get paid and paid well. Bad move on her part, a very bad move. I disposed of her badly beaten corpse. I didn't know that she had left evidence with her relatives. In the event of her sudden disappearance, they were to turn the evidence over to the police. That's what they did.

Months after my arrest, bodies were still being found. I was on the cover of numerous national and international magazines. My Asia was reunited with her real parents. She still loved me. She didn't hold anything against me. She visits me quite often. We talk about life and it's many choices. My choice is to get out of this place and administer some good old fashioned payback. My lawyer keeps telling me to be good and wait for my release. I don't think so. I have to finish off the people that are responsible for my incarceration. Then maybe I can finish raising my Asia.

6. OLD PEOPLE

Getting old is not something that people think about very often. We take life for granted and we think we will live forever. Most people are not prepared for old age. We are always searching for ways to look and feel younger, searching for a fountain of youth. When reality hits, bad back, gray hair, arthritis, failing eyesight, it's too late to plan and prepare. If we are lucky enough to live a long life, we should count our blessings. Aging is a very natural process. When aging is premature or unnatural, we become very concerned. What do we do when we age before our time?

Whomever finds this diary, read it very carefully. There are not a lot of answers but it should be helpful to you. Remember to enjoy life and treasure all the things that life has to offer you. day one: Today, my family and I, moved to a little country town just outside of New England. My father got a better job opportunity and had to relocate. I miss all of my friends already. I hope to meet new friends here. My little brother and my little sister are eager to go out and explore our new surroundings. I have had to help raise my siblings every since my mother passed away two years ago. I am seventeen years old and a recent high school graduate. After the summer ends, I will attend college. We have a whole lot of unpacking to do. After we unpack, we will probably go to bed. It is getting pretty late and we are all very tired. We'll check things out in the morning. day two: I love Saturday mornings. I made a really nice breakfast for my family. My dad left to go and visit his new office building. After we finish our breakfast, my brother, sister, and I will explore the town. Maybe we can meet some new friends. I did not see any kids when we drove into town. All I saw was old people. No middle aged people, no teenagers, no kids, just old people. I know where kids were, though. The first place that we went to was the park. There wasn't a kid in sight, there were just a few senior citizens out riding the swings and walking about. The old people around here sure do have a lot of energy. Our next stop was the arcade. Once again, no kids, just senior citizens. This place seems to be upside down. Maybe the kids are at the places where the old people are supposed to be. We checked the bingo halls and the nursing homes, no kids anywhere. We decided to try again tomorrow.

We walked home. I told my brother and my sister that all of the kids might be at camp. day three: Dad got in late last night. He looks different today. He looks older. His normally jet black hair has streaks of gray in it. We were supposed to go to church today but dad says that he is too tired to take us. We were dissappointed because church reminded us of our mother. I can still visualize her in the choir stand singing away. We went looking for other kids. After a couple of hours without any luck, we returned home. My brother and sister didn't look so good. They said that they were very tired. Two old men were sitting on our front porch. I thought that they were some of my father's new friends. I asked them if they were waiting for my dad. One of the old men stood up and said that he was my dad. I told him that he was not funny. He then preceded to tell me things that my dad only knew. I moved closer to get a better look at him. My God!! This old geezer was my dad. I asked him what had happened to him. He told me that he was too weak to talk. He instructed me to take my brother and sister inside and to put them in their beds. He told me to get some sleep and that he would tell me everything in the morning. Get some sleep? Get some sleep? How was I going to get some sleep while my dad was aging and my brother and sister were ill? day four: I tossed and turned all night. I might have gotten a couple of hours worth of sleep, between nightmares. I woke up with the chills. The house was empty. Where was everybody? I thought that I was having another nightmare. I smacked myself to see if I was sleep. I was wide awake because it hurt when I smacked myself. I called out to my family members but nobody responded. I was startled by the loud ringing of the doorbell. Very cautiously, I went to the door and I peeped thru the peephole in the front door. The old man who had been sitting on on the front porch yesterday, with my dad, was outside ringing the doorbell. I asked him what did he want. He said that he needed to talk to me about my family. Reluctantly, I let him inside. He said that his name was Ray. Ray started telling me a very strange story. Five days ago, Raymond was just another sixteen year old school boy. One evening, while mowing the yard, Ray saw a very bright light streaking across the sky. While looking at the light, Ray felt a strange tingle go thru his body. Everything went black and Ray passed out. When he came to, he was old. Everybody in town was old. The light had changed everybody. The people that were already old disintegrated into thin air. The mayor put the entire town under quarantine. Nobody could leave town and no outsiders could enter. Doctors and scientist tried in vain to find an explanation. They tried to find a cure. The food and the drinking water tested negative to any kind of contamination. At a town meeting, everybody voted to allow a few outsiders into town to see if they would turn old too. My father, my brother, and my sister were definitely affected. In the middle of the night, they were taken away to the hospital for tests and observation. I, for some reason, was unaffected by this phenomenon. After hearing Ray's story, I started screaming at him to take me to my family. day five: I have been traveling for a few years now. Dad told me to leave that town of old people and to never look back. I don't know where I am going or what I am going to do. Maybe I should go to college and become a scientist and try to find reasons for strange things. Whatever I do, I will never forget my family and the tragic events in that town. The only thing that I know for sure, for certain is that I will never take time for granted, I will appreciate each and every moment because the reality is, we are all getting older..

WEIRD SHORT STORIES

7. OUT OF BODY

The loud sound of sirens roaring deep into the night, flashing lights light up the dark sky, and I am awakened from a very peaceful sleep. I reach for my lovely wife, Debra Ann, but she is not there. She usually wakes me up when she awakens before I do. I love my wife with all my heart. Making love to my Debra Ann was almost like a religious experience. Last night we made love until we both passed out. Where could she be? The bedroom is smoky and hazy. Either the house is on fire or my glaucoma is acting up. I get out from under the covers and find myself fully dressed. This is very strange because I always sleep butt naked. There is a loud knock at my door. Who could be visiting at this time of night? I open the door and a flood of bright yellow light pours into my house. The light is coming from a yellow cab parked in my driveway. The driver is a spooky looking fellow. He tells me that he is here to pick me up and take me to see my wife. We leave my house. My car is gone and my wife's car is gone too. With both vehicles gone, I had to ride with the cabbie. I turned to go back into the house to get cab fare. The cab driver grabbed my arm and told me that we were running out of time. We both got into the cab and the cab driver drove off. We approach the scene of an accident. A fire truck and an ambulance are there with sirens blasting and lights flashing. Even though it is a bitter cold night, sweat pours down my forehead. I am shocked to find that it is my car that has been destroyed in this horrible accident. My car was a mangled mess, sitting on it's top, by the side of the road. I tell the cabbie to stop the cab so that I can find out what has happened. The cabbie keeps on driving and tells me that we don't have time, my wife is waiting for me. That was good news, she wasn't in that accident involving my car. She must have driven her own car. Apparently, somebody stole my car and wrecked it.

I must have dosed off. I woke up to find that the cab was parked and that the cab driver was gone. The cab was parked in the driveway of a very large mansion. It was very gothic looking. I heard the beautiful sound of gospel music coming from the mansion. I got out of the cab and walked towards the mansion and the gospel music that was coming from within the mansion. The closer I got, the louder the gospel music became. When I got to the doorway, I found that there were two white Bengal tigers guarding two golden doors. The doors opened and I entered the mansion. Inside of the mansion, there were no rooms, no walls, no ceiling, and no furniture. The inside of the mansion was a garden of flowers, Roses and Forget-Me-Nots. There was a pathway that went up a hill. I walked up the hill. On the other side of the hill there was nothing but pure hell. The gospel music was replaced by screams of torment and despair. The pathway was covered with spiders and scorpions. Raging fires burned on each side of the pathway. I kept on walking. At the end of the pathway, sitting alone crying, was my wife, Debra Ann. I tried to call to her but I could not speak. When I got close enough to her, I tried to touch her but I could not. The cab driver appeared, dressed like a doctor. He talked with Debra Ann but all I could hear was mumbling. She stopped crying and listened carefully to what the cab driver/ doctor had to say. He took my Debra Ann by the hand and led her up the pathway. They went right by me as if I wasn't even there. They disappeared over the hill. I ran after them. When I got to the top of the hill, I was pulled downward into a freefall. Faster and faster I fell for what seemed an eternity. I closed my eyes and prepared for the worst. I came to a sudden stop and I opened my eyes to a blinding light.

Here I lay, covered by wires and tape, strapped to a hospital bed. Sitting beside me is my wife, Debra Ann. She holds my hand and kisses it tenderly. The cab driver/ doctor enters the room and asks how I am feeling. I am pretty drugged up so it is hard to answer. I shake my head slowly up and down. I managed to ask him if we were in an accident while he was driving me in his cab. A puzzled look appeared on his face. He tells me that he hasn't driven a cab in over twenty years. He put himself through college by driving a yellow cab. He asked me how did I know about his cab driving days.

Three weeks in the hospital is no picnic. I am so glad to finally be back home. I don't remember a whole lot about my car accident. I was on my way to meet my wife. There was gospel music playing on the radio. The next thing I know, my car is flipping over and over. I was being surrounded by a smoky haze as my mangled car started burning. I was pulled from my car and I blacked out. That's all that I can remember. I was being worked on in the ambulance when I flat lined. I had died right then and there. I was revived at the hospital My body may fully recover some day, but my mind, that's another story. I don't know exactly what I experienced that day, but I know that I will never forget it.

8. TELEPHONE LOVE

We met over the telephone, by accident. A simple misdialing of a number that I had dialed hundreds of times before. It was my best friend John's telephone number. The phone rang three times. A soft and soothing voice answered. The voice was unfamiliar to me. It was the voice of an angel. I listened as she spoke. Hello, Alexus speaking, may I help you? I hesitated for a moment then I asked to speak to John. She told me that I had the wrong number because she did not know anybody called John. One thing led to another and before you know it, we were having a conversation.

Words are very powerful tools. There is an old nursery rhyme that says that sticks and stones may brake your bones but words can never hurt you. That's not true at all. Words can hurt you very bad. Words can get you killed. Words like; It's over, I hate you, I'm cheating on you, and even worse. Then again, there are words that can make you feel on top of the world. Those are the kind of words that Alexus and I spoke to each other.

Alexus was a very deep individual. She was very unlike the many bubble heads that I had been dating. She left London two years ago to come to the U.S. and make a new life for herself. She had been married to a very unfaithful man. She divorced him and came here. She described herself as being biracial, tall, and built with an hour glass figure. She had no kids and did not know if she wanted to have any kids or not. She had a masters degree in business and had just started her own business. She had been pouring all of her time and effort into her business. She had not dated since her divorce. She told me that she was glad to finally talk to a man that could hold a decent and intelligent conversation. She told me that I had a very sexy voice. I listened to every word that she spoke. Her English accent was very charming and it turned me on. I am not a very talkative person. In fact, I hardly ever talk on the telephone, but I held up my end of the conversation. I told this complete stranger all about myself.

When it comes to women, I am very picky. My friends tell me that I am very superficial. I do admit, sometimes I get very caught up in a woman's looks. If I meet a woman with what I call, bad genes, I try to ditch her as quick as I can. I am oblivious to my own imperfections. I

49

like my women to be perfect physical and mentally. No corns on the feet or pimples on the face. So why am I so nuts about somebody that I have never seen? She could be very beautiful or very ugly. I must be changing, maturing, because I am not concerned about how Alexus looks. I just know how good she sounds.

We began our telephone relationship, talking to each other once a week, usually at the end of the week. We both had more time and more things to say at the end of a week. We talked about any and everything. We continued this routine for a couple of months. We were becoming addicted to each other and we decided to converse more often. We talked to each other every other day. Finally, we were calling each other everyday. Sometimes we talked two or three times a day. We were enthralled by each other. She fascinated me, and I fascinated her. Our many conversations were like powerful, addictive drugs, and we both needed our daily fix.

Before we could stop it, we were madly in love. We put off meeting each other because we were both afraid to meet in person. I had developed a fairy tale image of what she looked like. She had her own fantasy of what I looked like. I guess that we both did not want to be disappointed. We did not want to find out that we finally found love and that we were not attracted to each other. Besides, the mystery of not knowing what each other looked like, was part of the attraction between us. We started having very intense phone sex. It was almost as satisfying as the real thing.

We carried on this way for months. Then it happened. Call it fate or call it destiny. We finally met in person. It wasn't planned. It happened totally by accident. I wanted to have Lasagna for dinner but I was out of pasta. I was out of wine too. I decided to run to the store so I could get back home in time to talk with Alexus. The store was crowded that day. I got my pasta and stood in line to pay for it. I remembered that I was out of wine so I got out of line and went looking for a bottle of quality wine. There, in the wine aisle, was a true vision of loveliness. If I was not in love with Alexus, I would have tried to pick up that beauty. I decided that it would not hurt to ask her which wine was the best to serve with Lasagna. As I approached her, she was trying to find a bottle of wine too. I asked her if she knew which vintage of wine would go best with Lasagna. She looked at me in astonishment. In her sexy voice, she said my name. There was no need for conversation, we had talked enough over the telephone. We hugged each other, standing in the middle of the aisle. Then we kissed.

After forty years of marital bliss, kids and grandkids, we are still very much in love. Like any couple, we have had our ups and we have had our downs. The very thing that brought us together, is the very same thing that keeps us together. We love to talk to each other.

9. I, MURDERER

I have always felt that life is very sacred. Nobody has a right to take a life. We can't create life so we have no right to destroy life. I have spent most of my life trying to preserve life. I support life saving organizations. I put up bird houses and bird feeders in my yard. I am a sponsor to poor children who live in poverty around the world. I am a Right to Life activist too. The thought of taking a life, makes me sick to my stomach, it repulses me. I can't serve in the armed forces because of my belief, it would be impossible. However, today I have murdered.

It all started yesterday morning. My kitchen garbage can had gotten full. When I took my garbage outside, my humble little home was invaded. An uninvited guest followed me inside my home. Being the caring and patient person that I am, I allowed the intruder to stay. As long as it behaved itself, it could enjoy all of the comfort my home had to offer. My guest was very sneaky. It chose to hide around my house while it made bothersome noises. This behavior was not appropriate. I was getting annoyed. I was frustrated and bothered in my own home. Taking a peaceful nap was impossible. My patience began to ware thin. I started seeing this uninvited guest as a moocher and a common vagrant. I had hoped that my body language would convey my unhappiness to the intruder. Then the intruder would take the hint and leave on it's own. It did not leave. It got louder and even more bothersome. Something had to be done right away. I had been a very good host and I had been taken advantage of.

My patience ran out. I decided to take some extreme measures. I planned each step very carefully. I left no room for error. This had to be done and I didn't want anybody to find out about it. I wouldn't get many chances because the intruder was very crafty, very stealth. For a couple of hours, we played the game of cat and mouse. I was having second thoughts but I continued on with the plan. Deep inside of me was a killer waiting to awaken. The sleeper had awakened and there was no turning back.

Finally I spotted the intruder. We both made eye contact. The intruder attempted to hypnotize me but I was able to shake it off. I made sure that there were no escape routes available to the intruder.

The intruder fully understood what I had planned for it. The intruder started pacing back and forth, looking for a way out. With cat like reflexes, that I didn't know that I possessed, I sprang into action. It was over quickly. I can still hear that horrible sound, splat!! Body parts were intertwined in a mixture of death. The smell of death filled the air. A feeling of dread came over me. I had to dispose of the evidence and I had to do it fast. Visitors might show up and discover that I have killed.

I took the dead remains of the intruder outside to my backyard. I dug a hole to bury the dead remains of the intruder. I buried all of the evidence. The hairs on my neck stiffened up. I felt like I was being watched. I said a few words over the grave, and returned inside of my home. My head was filled with guilt and anxiety. What if the intruder had a family to care for? Why did I, a crusader for life, act like a murderous barbarian? Where was my compassion? Where was my zest for life? I thought about going to confession but I felt uncomfortable with the fact that someone would know about me, even a priest.

The next day, I heard noises. It was the same sound made by the intruder, but louder. Perhaps it was the intruder's family coming to get revenge. If it was, I was more than ready for them. I had killed before so killing again would not be a problem. This is my house. I pay the bills here. I will not be intruded upon in my own house. What am I saying? What has gotten into me? I am not a cold blooded killer. I must stay in control. Maybe I can reason with them.

I have killed again. It was so easy. They never saw me coming. I didn't even bother with a burial this time. They forced my hand. They made me kill again. They should have just left me alone. I have changed from being a gentle and docile person, to being a murderer. There must be a murderer inside each of us. When circumstances allow, it appears. All morals are repressed. You don't care anymore about right and wrong. All of my friends and associates think of me as someone who wouldn't hurt a fly. Today, I hurt a lot of flies. Today I murdered.

10. CASANOVA BROWN

Six feet two inches, two hundred pounds of rippling muscle, naturally curly jet black hair, dark brown hypnotic eyes, unmarked chocolate skin, this was Casanova Brown. Most women wanted to date him while most men wanted to be like him. Casanova Brown was a very successful man. Whatever he tried, he was good at it. With success comes ego and Casanova Brown had plenty of ego. Casanova was in love with himself and himself only. Women were seen by Casanova Brown as merely playthings for his amusement. He was not very choosy about the women that he went out with, he treated them all the same, like they were dirt. As long as they had plenty of money to spend on him, as long as they worshipped the ground that he walked on, the ladies could spend time with him, the great Casanova Brown. He was so smooth that the ladies didn't even know that he was just using them, toying with them. Maybe they just didn't care. Ladies were entranced by Casanova's charm. Once Casanova made eye contact, very few females could resist him. The true essence of his charisma, was his smile. Casanova had thirty two perfect teeth and he knew how to flash them. He was a gigolo, a playboy, and he lived a very expensive lifestyle. He would never let anybody get too close to him. He enjoyed being free and single. He had never loved anybody but himself, until he met Lorain.

There was a song written called "SWEET LORAIN". That song was most likely written about Casanova's Lorain. She had just gotten off the train, having traveled all the way from New Orleans. She was a vision of loveliness. Lorain checked into the very hotel that Casanova Brown owned. Lorain caught the eye of Casanova Brown. He had to have her. He pursued Lorain relentlessly. You might even say that he stalked her, but in a very classy way. The more she ignored him, the more that she rebuffed him, only made him more determined to win her affection. It seems that we all want what we can not have. Casanova's tremendous ego was taking a pounding. Eventually, Lorain gave in and allowed Casanova to date her. He took Lorain to expensive restaurants, trying to impress her, but she was not impressed. Casanova showered Lorain with expensive gifts. This did not impress her either. They dated for weeks and Lorain wouldn't even let Casanova hold her hand. She was dogging the dog. Casanova was so infatuated with Lorain, he didn't notice that his bank account was vanishing. When his money was getting low, he could no longer buy Lorain expensive gifts and take her to very expensive restaurants. Lorain decided that it was time for her to leave. Casanova begged Lorain to stay, or to let him come with her. She ignored his begging. His plea fell on deaf ears. Lorain left Casanova crying, like a baby, at the airport.

Six months went by. Casanova snapped out of the funk that he was in and became his old self again. He was dating a different lady every night. Lorain was a distant memory. One Sunday morning, Casanova woke up and found himself handcuffed to his bed. Sitting at the end of the bed, Indian style, was Lorain. She was wearing a tight, sexy, black catsuit. She wore a Lone Ranger mask too. In her left hand was a black rose. In her right hand was a high voltage stun gun. She had her head bowed and she appeared to be in a trance. Casanova, in a startled state, asked Lorain what was going on. Lorain came out of her trance, lifted her head and screamed like a crazy person. She smacked Casanova upside the head with the black rose. She held the stun gun high in the air and shouted at Casanova, "Sampson, the Philistines be upon you". Lorain brought the stun gun down on Casanova's big toe. Casanova's body gyrated in a frenzied state as the electricity traveled from his toe to his head. Casanova passed out. When he came to, he found himself butt naked, covered in oil, and strapped to a lazy boy chair. Lorain was sitting on the floor, directly across from Casanova. Casanova cried out, "What's your problem you crazy bitch?". Lorain laughed out loud and told Casanova that she did not have a problem. He was the one tied up and being tortured, he had the problem. She called Casanova a cheating, lying, punk. She told Casanova that he needed to be punished. Lorain pulled out a bull whip and whipped Casanova like he was a caught runaway slave. Once again, he passed out. When he came too, Lorain was gone. When Casanova screamed for help, the door to his suite flung open. A very pretty, middle aged lady stood in the doorway. She asked Casanova if he remembered her. She was one of Casanova's ex-lovers. In fact, he had just dumped her only a few weeks before he met Lorain. Casanova thanked her for coming to his aid and begged her to untie him and to call for some help. She told Casanova that she didn't come to rescue him. She came to make sure that he got what he had coming to him. She told Casanova that after he dumped her, she almost committed suicide. Her brother saved her and promised to help her to get some payback from Casanova. Lorain entered the suite and hugged the vengeful lady. The vengeful lady told Casanova that this was her baby brother. Casanova shouted that Lorain wasn't nobody's brother, she was all woman. With a big smile, Lorain whipped out Mister Happy. Lorain was indeed a man.

Casanova was released but he was never the same after that ordeal. Both his ego and his manhood had become traumatized. The world was no longer his playpen. He developed a brand new respect for all women. He understood that a woman was unique and powerful. He had experienced that power up close and personal. He learned that disrespecting women could lead to some very severe repercussions. When he was a gigolo, he caused many women to shed many tears. In those days, he never thought once about the pain that he was causing. He had only thought about the money, sex, and attention that he was getting. One revenge filled encounter changed the thinking of the mighty Casanova Brown.

Casanova changed his name back to his birth name, Thomas Andrew Brown. He enrolled in city college and pursued a degree in Sociality. He changed the way that he talked and the way that he walked. No more fancy clothes or expensive jewelry for him. He still thinks of himself as a lover though. In fact, you will most likely find Mr. Brown in one of the neighborhood gay bars. His new admiration and respect for women, made him want to be like a woman. He has truly gotten in touch with his feminine side.

11. BUBBLE CHILD

Little Kinney was born prematurely. Don't call him a preemie, he hates that. On the day of his birth, a lot of strange things happened. Lightning lit up the sky, golf ball size hail fell from the sky, and all of the clocks stopped keeping time. All of the power went off. When the power came back on, there was Little Kenney, sleeping in his mother's arms. Little Kinney was born premature and had a lot of ailments to deal with. There was always some unexplained illness that was followed by another unexplained illness. He was a bubble child. Along with all of the sickness, came a special gift. That gift was the ability to hear what people were thinking. He was not a mind reader but he could definitely hear thoughts. He could only hear one person at a time, and only when he concentrated on that one person. Little Kenney's parents are the only people who knew about his gift. They think that all of the medications that Little Kenney has had to take over the years are the cause of this phenomenon.

Both of Little Kenney's parents are school teachers. They love their son very dearly. They never thought that they could have children. To them, Little Kenney is a blessing from heaven. Little Kenney's fragile heath did not allow him to attend regular school. His parents took turns home schooling him. When his parents had to be away, his grandmother took care of him. Little Kenney's parents knew that with the right care and with a lot of love, Little Kenney would outgrow his fragile physical state. They knew that he would get stronger and that he would no longer be a bubble child. Little Kenney never got to play with other kids. He was not allowed outside. He had never rode a bike, a scooter, or a skateboard. He would look out of his window and watch the neighborhood kids. These kids were playing, fighting, laughing, and crying. These are the things that normal kids were participating in. During times like these, Little Kenney felt sad. He felt like he was missing out on all of these experiences. Sometimes the other kids could see Little Kenney looking out of the window. They would wave and motion for him to come outside and join them. Little Kenney wanted to, but his fragile body was not ready for the physicality of playing outside.

On his tenth birthday, Little Kenney's parents asked him what he wanted for a present. He told his parents that the only present that he wanted was to be able to go outside and play. Little Kenney was not so little any more. He had been getting bigger and stronger every year. His immune system was becoming normal. Little Kenney's parents knew that it would mean a lot to him to be able to go outside and play. They gave Little Kenney the birthday present that he had asked for. He was allowed to go outside for an hour but he was not allowed to leave the fenced in yard. Every fifteen minutes or so, one of his parents would come out and check on Little Kenney. His grandmother came out and sat on the porch, in her rocking chair. She kept her eye on him. Little Kenney was both excited and scared at the same time. At first, he was content to just sit on the porch and observe. The neighborhood kids began to fill up the street. Little Kenney wanted to join them but he was held back by his grandmother. She reminded him to stay within the fenced in yard. She told him to take it slow and easy. Some of the kids noticed Little Kenney. They ran to the fence to meet him. They asked him what his name was and why he stayed in the house all of the time. Little

Kenney told them his name. He told them that he had a bad immune system and had been very sickly since the day that he was born. Today was his birthday and he was allowed to go outside. The kids invited Little Kenny to play kickball with them. He told them that he was not allowed to leave the yard and that he did not know how to play any games. They told Little Kenney to watch them and he could learn how to play kickball that way.

Little Kenney's hour outside came and went with no complications. His parents were very happy and decided to let Little Kenney play outside more often. When Little Kenney was outside watching the neighborhood kids playing, some very disturbing thoughts were coming into Little Kenney's head. He was getting the thoughts of the neighborhood kids and found out that some of these kids were in trouble. Some very bad things were happening to theses kids. Playing outside was their only escape. One little girl was in a very abusive home environment. She needed help and she was planning to run away from home. A little boy was being used by his drug dealing stepfather to drop off drugs. There were a lot more stories like these. Little Kenney wanted to help these kids. Little

Kenney asked his parents if they knew that kids attending their school were being abused. Then he asked his parents how to go about helping abused kids. Little Kenney's parents wondered why their son would ask such questions. They tried to answer his questions as honestly and completely as possible. They told their son about the different agencies that were formed to protect children. They told their son that if they knew of any abused children, they would write to the child protection agencies. That is exactly what Little Kenney did.

Months had passed since Little Kenney had started his letter writing crusade. One day, while reading the newspaper at breakfast, Little Kenney's dad spotted an article about the local government's crackdown on child abuse. Local government officials stated in the article, that an unidentified citizen had reported about cases of child abuse throughout the area. Little Kenney's father turned and looked at his son with a very proud expression. He did not have to say a word. Little Kenney was hearing his thoughts.

At the age of twelve, Little Kenney was officially freed from his bubble. He went on to graduate at the top of his class. He went to a very good college and graduated with honors. He pursued a law degree and was very successful doing that too. He used his special gift to help abused children. He tired of law and began his own private detective agency. He earned fame and fortune by solving the unsolvable. With his money, he invested in lots of medical research companies. He wanted a cure for all kinds of childhood diseases and defects. The thought of a child having to live in a bubble like he did, made Little Kenney angry and upset. He thought that enough research was not being done.

As a grown man, Little Kenney became known simply as Kenneth. He had outgrown the name Little Kenney. Through his research grants, he came to know a very special female doctor. They fell in love with each other. Just like Kenneth, she had been a bubble child. Her childhood sickness left her deaf and partially blind. Like Kenneth, she had a special gift, a six sense. They became husband and wife. Together, they made a great team. Eventually, they had a baby. It was a baby boy. Unlike his parents, the baby boy was born healthy, too healthy. He was born with super human strength and intelligence. One of the doctors at the hospital where the baby was born, also worked for government research. This doctor told some of his research associates about the baby boy. There was a plot put into place, a plot to steal Kenneth's baby boy and do research on him. They were going to tell Kenneth and his wife, that the baby developed complications and died. Together, Kenneth and his wife, with their special gifts, caught on to the plot to take their son. They found their son and escaped with him deep into the woods. There was a big search for them but they evaded capture. Kenneth, his wife, and his baby boy, ended up on top of a high hill in the middle of the woods. A force coming from deep within them led them to the hilltop. They were huddled close together in a loving embrace. Suddenly, out of nowhere, came a bright flashing light. They had vanished into thin air. They were going home.

12. MANSTERS

The word monster, has many definitions. On planet Earth, the only true monsters are human beings. Man, created to care for and to nurture the Earth, has done nothing but destroy and pollute the Earth. Even though Man was created with the power of intelligence and the gift of reasoning, Man shows nothing but a total disregard for life and it's beauty. Man systematically destroys all other species, along with him or herself. Using technology, science, and religion, Man has wiped out entire cultures and civilizations. Man is truly the only monster. Beware of the Mansters.

Mansters are not born, they are created and developed by evil forces. Parents teach their children how to become full fledged Mansters. Mansters live by a special set of principles. Mansters make the law, therefore, Mansters are the law. Laws were created to be broken. Those with the biggest guns rule. If you are not a Manster, you have no rights.

It is the year 2310. Mansters are looking for me. I do not remember offending them in any manner. They can't be reasoned with. They defy both knowledge and reason. I don't look or dress like them. Maybe that is why they are after me. Maybe they are after me because of the way that I worship the Creator. Is it my politics? It really does not matter. All that matters is that they are looking for me and I can't allow them to find me. Can they be stopped? Maybe they can be stopped, maybe they can not. All I know is that if they find me, they will try to change me or they will kill me.

They hide in the woods, in dark alleys, at entertainment venues. They are Board Chairman, School Principle, Church member, etc.. Deception is their weapon of choice. They travel the world, looking for new members or new victims. If you have something that they want, they will take it from you. They are driven by fear. Whatever they fear, they destroy. They are not the masters of there own fate because they fear the unknown. They fear other people's knowledge. They pass out leaflets that say that the Earth belongs to them and that it is their birthright to dictate all that happens on the Earth. Most Mansters acknowledge the Creator even though they ignore the laws of the Creator. Still, there are some Mansters that think that they created themselves or simply evolved.

There is a Manster within each of us, trying to get out. I am not a Manster yet, but I can feel it inside of me trying to come forward. It has taken most of my strength and energy to keep it in check. Mansters have been trying to change me for quite a while. They come at me from all angles, trying to convert me to their way of thinking. I have fought a brave fight. I have fought long and hard but I can feel them closing in. I don't have a lot of time left.

Mankind is always looking for the next catastrophe, the next plague. All they have to do is to look in the mirror. The plague is already here. Man destroys all of the trees and grasslands, creating concrete jungles. Commerce and land development replace conservation. Mansters are leaving a legacy of war, famine, disease, overpopulation, and total disregard of nature. Is the death of Man the only way to stop Mansters? Maybe that is the only way that the Earth can survive. All Mansters are well aware that the destruction of the Earth is eminent. They don't care. Maybe that's why they keep exploring space. They want to find another Earth, other beings to destroy. They fear the unknown. Life on other planets is the unknown. If beings from other planets visit the Earth, they had better be in fear for their lives. Mansters shoot first and ask questions later. Much, much later. If Mansters were to find an inhabitable planet, they would take it. If the planet was inhabited by intelligent beings, Mansters would simply draw up a treaty or official looking document. A worthless peace of paper. They would do the same thing that The Colonist did to the Indians. Get them drunk, high, or both, and have them make their mark on the dotted line. Any resistors would be killed or put on reservations.

Oh no!! They have found my hiding place. When it comes to Mansters, there are no hiding places, no safe havens, no sanctuary. They are upon me. They have me. I have become one of them. Greed, lust, and hatred are taking control of me and I like it. I plan to become a member of all the local hate groups. Hell, I'll just go out and form my own hate group. We'll hate everybody, including each other. When you are a Manster, there are no limitations, no moral issues to hold you back. There is no higher power to answer to. I have to make up for lost time. There are churches and clinics to bomb, forest fires to set, and people to kill. All of that goody two shoes nonsense that I was talking, forget all of that. Forget the person that I once was. Always remember, Mansters Rule!!!!

13. CLOWNS

A Clown is defined as a performer in a circus, carnival, birthday party, or a pantomime who entertains, as by joke or tricks; court jester. Clowns come in many different sizes and shapes. They usually dress in oversized baggy clothes, oversized floppy shoes, and sometimes a floppy hat. Their hair is usually long and brightly colored. They have an unforgettable large red button nose along with a painted on smile. Some are silent, just like mimes. Others are loud with silly, goofy laughs. They come off as goofy, duffy, clumsy, oafs. They have a clown name like Bobo, Bozo, Lucky, Jojo, etc... They try to keep your attention and to captivate you by performing various antics and practical jokes. Clowns are born to be pranksters. Their jokes are usually funny, unless the joke is on you. Some of their standard gimmicks are pie throwing, flowers squirting, throwing buckets of confetti, bursting balloons, etc... Sometimes a small vehicle drives to center ring and out jumps more clowns than the vehicle should be able to hold. It's truly an amazing sight.

Clowns, tents, popcorn, and cotton candy mean one thing. The circus is coming to town. I love a good circus but I hate the clowns. I usually get some free tickets whenever the circus comes to town, but I never go. I know that those clowns will be there so I give my tickets away. Clowns are so fake and phony. Their smiles are simply frowns turned upside down. Clowns scare the hell out of me. I don't buy into their harmless fun pretense. I know exactly what they are capable of doing. Clowns are not the happy go lucky goofballs that they pretend to be. They are evil. They hide behind the make-up and funny looks to fool the people.

Paranoia is a very strange disease. It can affect the strong as well as the weak. When you are paranoid, it is hard to tell the difference between what is fact and what is fiction. Reality and imagination become one. Your deepest fears come to the forefront and take you on an uncontrollable ride of fear. Clowns make me paranoid.

Jason, Michael Myers, Freddy, are names of fictional killers that wore masks, make-up, or both, to hide and conceal what they were and who they were. Clowns have been around for a much longer time and they are real, not fictional characters in a book or movie. I have both feared and hated clowns since the age of six. I can still remember my first encounter with clowns.

My mother was given free passes to go and attend the local circus. I had never been to the circus. Mother thought that I would like the circus so she took me to see it. It was great, at first. I remember the big balloons, the fresh smell of buttered popcorn, and eating cotton candy that melted inside of my mouth. I can still see all of the people, smiling and enjoying themselves. It was both fun and strange at the same time. There were three circles. Each circle or ring had some kind of event going on. One circle had people riding gigantic bikes. Another circle featured a lady in her undies, riding a big white horse. A man with a chair and a whip was inside of a cage filled with giant cats. Overhead, there were some people walking from one end of a little wire to the other end. There were monkeys riding elephants too. It was all very new to me and I did not want to miss any of it. Little did I know that my fun was about to come to an end. A little red car drove to center ring. It stopped right in front of my mother and I. We had ringside seats. Five really big clowns jumped out of this little red car. The people in the audience were going crazy over this. The clowns started to mess with the people in the audience, especially the kids. The clowns were looking for a volunteer from the audience. All of the kids, except me, raised their hands and were going nuts. I wanted no part of this. I remember thinking to myself, I got to get the hell out of here. I asked my mother to take me to the restroom. Before she could get me out of there, one of those clowns snatched me out of my seat. Out of the hundreds of willing volunteers, they chose the most bewildered little kid in the whole audience, me. I started screaming at the top of my lungs. I was filled with terror. Nobody would help me, they were too busy laughing. The clowns placed my fear filled body on top of the little red car. The clowns started dancing around the little red car. They did back flips and summmersaults, driving the crowd even more frenzied. They scared me so bad that poo popped out of my butt and down my pants leg. Their painted faces and their creepy yellow teeth, terrorized me. I knew that I had to make a move and make it quick. I summoned up what little courage that I had left and jumped off of the little red car. I ran as fast as my little legs could carry me. It took the police almost six hours to find me. My mother told me she was sorry and tried to console me, to

78

calm me down. Those horrible smiling faces have given me nightmares every since that day.

When I reached adulthood, I decided that I was going to make a change in my life. I was tired of the nightmares and the fear. I decided that I was going to turn the tables on those clowns. Instead of me fearing them, I was going to make them fear me. I started off by following clowns home from work, the circus, a birthday party, etc... Then I would beat the hell out of them. Pretty soon, nobody in town wanted to work as a clown. There was a city wide panic among clowns. Even clowns from out of town refused to come here to work. I finally eliminated my fear. Now it's about time for all clowns to live with fear for awhile.

14. RESTRAINING ORDER

I have known and worked with Wilbur for a few years now. In my opinion, Wilbur needs some serious counseling. Even though we work together, we are not buddies. For some reason, he liked to talk to me. Sometimes it was boring and at other times, it was very entertaining. Wilbur liked to bring his personal business to work with him. Most of it was about his wife and kids. He needed somebody to confide in and I guess that I was the lucky or the unlucky one. I did not believe most of the things that he told me. If any of it was true, he needed to seek some professional help. Sometimes, Wilbur gave me the creeps.

Wilbur loved being married. He had been married four times so I figured that he must have loved being married. Wilbur would bring pictures of his current wife to work with him. She was young and she was beautiful. What was she doing with Wilbur? It seemed to me that she knew how to upset Wilbur and that she enjoyed doing it. Wilbur would sometimes report to work in a confused daze. He would mope around and cry. He would tell whoever he could about his problems. That usually meant me. Wilbur's wife would upset him by wearing sexy clothes like mini dresses and tight jeans. She had the body and she liked to show it off. Guys would whistle at her and Wilbur would get out of control. He would tell me that his wife dresses like a little skank. Wilbur loved his wife but he was very insecure and he was very jealous. He told me that he had made it clear to her that leaving him was out of the question. Eventually, Wilbur's wife got tired of him and filed for divorce. He would not let it go. He would not leave her alone so she had a Restraining Order filed against him. During our many conversations, Wilbur had neglected to tell me about his drinking binges and about the many beatings that he had administered to his wife. Like his previous wives, she was not going to stay with Wilbur and be his punching bag.

Wilbur came to work each day with his Restraining Order folded neatly inside of his shirt pocket. During breaks and during lunch, Wilbur would take the Restraining Order out of his pocket and stare at it, reading it over and over. I never told anyone but Wilbur told me that he kept a loaded gun in his car. This was starting to bother me.

Wilbur was getting worse each day. He would stand on a chair and shout cuss words at the top of his lungs. He would hold up the Restraining order and say it doesn't mean shit to him, and that no piece of paper could keep him from what was his. Needless to say, Wilbur violated the Restraining over again and again. His outburst were making everybody at work nervous, especially me. The company made him get help. Wilbur was put on medication. I don't think that he was taking his medication like he should. He was still acting the same as far as I could tell. Rumors and gossip were making their way around the workplace. Some of our fellow workers started making jokes about Wilbur. I remember one particular incident when Wilbur attacked one of the guys at work. He was joking about sleeping with Wilbur's wife and he called her a two dollar whore. It took six of us to pull Wilbur off of him. Wilbur was taken away in a straight jacket and given medical leave.

While on medical leave, Wilbur started plotting and planning. He spent hours surfing the internet. He bought disguises and surveillance equipment. He was becoming a professional stalker. I thought that he was going to hurt himself or somebody else. I called his wife and warned her about Wilbur and his many activities. She thanked me but she did not seem too concerned.

About a month later, I got a call from Wilbur's wife. Her home had been broken into while she was out. The alarm system had been disabled. The only things stolen were her sexy clothes. Somebody had stolen her clothes and replaced them with conservative dresses and pantsuits. Someone by the name of Wilbur, perhaps? She told me that the divorce had finally gone through and she asked me to tell Wilbur to stay away from her, or else. I gave him the message but he kept on stalking her. He used a variety of disguise but she knew that it was him. She bought herself a stun gun and some mace. She called me and told me that she was going to put an end to this game of cat and mouse. I told her to do what she felt she had to do.

About three months later, Wilbur came back to work. He was a changed man. He had a black eye, a broken nose, and he walked with a limp. He was very uptight and very jumpy. He was very paranoid, constantly looking over his shoulder. I asked him about what had happened to him. He started to cry but he regained his composure. He told me that he had been stalking his ex-wife. One day, while he was out stalking her, a van came out of nowhere and ran him down. Six people, wearing masks and disguises, jumped out of the van and gave him an ass whooping. They put him in the van, drove to a hospital and dumped his limp body out. They shouted two words to Wilbur before they drove off, Restraining Order. After a couple of weeks in the hospital, Wilbur started stalking his ex-wife again. The van came out of nowhere again and he was beaten pretty badly again. They drove Wilbur to the hospital, dumped him out of the van, and shouted the words, Restraining Order. After two severe ass kickings, Wilbur finally got the message. He learned to respect the Restraining Order.

15. GIRL TALK

My name is Isabella Marie. I am chief clinical psychiatrist at one of the best hospitals in the United States. When I am not working at the hospital, I am a part-time columnist for the local newspaper. I write a very successful advise column called, "ASK SHEILA". As a psychiatrist, I realize the various ways that people can be affected by columns like mine. I try to be non-personal and analytical. I give honest and straight forward advise. While I do have a staff to screen all of the letters, in the end, I have final say and approval.

I can still remember my first day on the job. The column was brand new. The general public had no knowledge of the new column. My staff made up letters until we got ourselves established. The real letters started pouring in. I knew that there were going to be some strange letters but I did not know how strange. In my field, I meet a lot of people with some very serious issues. Some of the people that were writing in to my column were no different than some of my mental patients. Most of them need more help than an advise column can give them. I do what I can to help them.

I try not to take my work home with me. Home is where you relax and try to get away from it all. However, most of the time, it can't be helped. Some of the letters that I have read have caused me many a sleepless night. One of my first letters was from a really troubled young lady. She called herself, "SIMPLY CONFUSED". Her letter went like this:

DEAR SHEILA,

A year ago I met a very nice guy. He was tall, dark, and handsome. He was a very polite gentleman and he was also very respectful. He was my dream come true, my fantasy guy. We became very good friends, then we began dating each other. We became lovers and for a while, we were inseparable. Our first couple of weeks together reminded me of the novel, "NINE AND ONE HALF WEEKS". We took intimacy to totally new levels. I'm talking incense, wine, and candles. There were foot massages, rim shots, sponge baths, etc... Sometimes he would prepare my favorite meal and hand feed me each morsel while I sat on his lap being grinded on. He called me everyday to find out how I was feeling. I felt like it was all too good to be true, and it was. His visits and his phone calls have been getting shorter and shorter. I feel like our relationship is changing, and not for the better. We had never discussed it but I was under the impression that we were both in love and that we were going to be husband and wife. Am I being unrealistic? Should I confront his ass about the situation?

SIMPLY CONFUSED

Nothing about this letter seemed out of the ordinary. There was no red flag signal being sent. She was a typical female product of our society. Most women want a fantasy guy in their life. I know that I surely do. Women meet a smooth talking man and fall in love. They hope that he, in turn, loves them in return. When that does not happen, they seek the answers to questions that they alone can answer. I thought that her problem and her solution was pretty simple. I answered her letter.

SIMPLY CONFUSED,

Communication is an essential part of any healthy relationship. Assuming that this man has no telepathic abilities, you need to sit down and talk with him. You need to know if he wants what you want. If what you want and what he wants are totally different things, then you need to make some serious decisions. Don't set yourself up for heartbreak.

SHEILA

I had hoped that she would move on with her life. One month later, SIMPLY CONFUSED wrote me another letter.

DEAR SHEILA,

I took your advise. I tried to pussywhip him just like you told me to. It did not work. I watched thousands of porno movies just like you advised, but I did not learn anything knew. I let him use and abuse me. I became his total sex slave, but he is still trying to play me. He stopped calling me so I call him twenty to thirty times a day. I went by his job to confront him but he had me removed from the premises. You told me that he was probably an ungrateful bastard but I did not believe you. I am having his baby just like you told me to. I need to know my next course of action, please advise.

SIMPLY CONFUSED

Crazy bitch!! This looney tune must have me confused with somebody else that she has been writing. I never told her to do anything but talk to her man and find what he wants out of the relationship. SIMPLY CONFUSED is more than simply confused. Needless to say, her letter was trashed and not published. I had hoped not to hear from her again. Two months later, she wrote me another letter.

DEAR SHEILA,

Your advise stinks. I should sue you and that stinking paper that you write for. You told me to stalk my man. You told me that he would come around to my way of thinking. It never happened. He has had me arrested on several occasions. I don't know what I ever saw in that weak sissy punk man. He made me so angry that I took your advise and burned down his house. I am getting ready to kidnap him like you told me and cut off his nuts. Please advise.

SIMPLY CONFUSED

I should have contacted the police. Maybe the police could have found this crazy lady and gotten her off the streets. I chose to ignore the letters. I figured that SIMPLY CONFUSED was probably just a harmless prankster trying to get some attention. After two months passed, I figured that everything was alright. Then it happened, my boss called me into his office. He had a very concerned look on his face. He told me that SIMPLY CONFUSED sent in another letter and that he read the letter. He gave me the letter, told me to read the letter and call the police afterwards. I read the letter.

DEAR SHEILA,

Everything is working out great for me. I joined the cult that you advised me to join. After we kidnapped and tortured my ex-boyfriend, I felt a lot better about things. I have enclosed one of his fingers, please preserve it for me. When I was one of your patients, your advise wasn't nearly as good. You go girl, keep up the good work. I am leaving the country with my new man so I won't be able to write to you anymore. Hugs and Kisses. P.S., I am sorry about stealing your

car but I know that you won't mind.

16. DADDY

The weekend is coming and Daddy, my stepfather is taking me to visit my father. Visiting my father is a complete waste of time and I hate to go. He doesn't act like a father at all. He is always gone somewhere and always leaves me with his mother. His mother, my grandmother, treats me pretty bad. There is no love and there is no family bonding. It is not a very good environment for a kid to grow up in, even for just a weekend.

Daddy married my mommy a few days after she found out that she was pregnant, expecting me. Daddy and my mommy had been friends for a long time. They were best friends. Prior to marrying each other, they had never officially dated, but they loved each other dearly. Mommy was a very pretty girl and always had men chasing after her. She would always compare other men to Daddy to size them up. If they did not compare favorably to Daddy, she would dump them. Each time that she would break up with somebody, she would come running to Daddy so that she could cry on his shoulder. The day that she broke up with my father, she came running back to Daddy to be consoled. Daddy always knew what to say to make mommy feel better, but this time things were different. This time they discovered their true feelings for each other. They made love like there was no tomorrow. Three weeks later, mommy found out that she was pregnant with me.

Daddy had been told by his doctor that he was sterile and that he could not make any babies. Daddy and mommy concluded that mommy's ex-boyfriend was my father. My father was told about the pregnancy. He did not want a baby. He told mommy to get an abortion. Mommy was hurt and confused. She broke down and started to cry. That's when Daddy proposed to her. That was fifteen years ago.

Three years after Daddy and mommy were married, my father decided that he wanted to be a father to me. He got together with a lawyer and tried to get custody of me. The court would not give him custody of me but they did give my father visitation rights. He was allowed to keep me every other weekend. It turns out that he had no intensions of being a father to me. He was just being jealous and spiteful. After all, this is the same person that told mommy to get an abortion.

Daddy was a real father to me. In fact, my very first word was Daddy. I would walk around all day saying Daddy. I loved Daddy as though he were my real father. He is my role model. He is my hero. When I get sick, it is Daddy that takes care of me or that takes me to the hospital. When there is a parent-teacher meeting or a P.T.A., Daddy is always there. Daddy spoils my mommy and me. Daddy makes sure that the bills are always paid and that there is always plenty of food to eat. Daddy treats my mommy like the queen that she is.

Every time that I visit my father, I always notice the fact that we look nothing alike. He is short and fair skinned. I am tall and dark skinned. Mommy is short and fair skinned just like my father. So why am I tall and dark? Now Daddy looked like me, tall and dark. I always wondered why Daddy and I looked so much alike.

On my fifteenth birthday, Daddy went to visit his grandmother and took me along to keep him company. Daddy had not seen his grandmother since he married mommy. It was a long five hour drive.

Daddy and I told jokes and stories to liven up the trip. We laughed all the way and the trip did not seem as long. Daddy's granny was very old. She was kind of crazy too. Her eyesight wasn't very good and she walked with the aid of a cane. When she came to the door and saw me, her eyes lit up like a Christmas tree. Inside of Daddy's granny's house, were walls covered with pictures. These pictures were of Daddy and his relatives. It felt kind of funny looking at these pictures because all of the pictures looked like me. It was like looking in a mirror. Daddy's granny fixed us some lunch. While we ate, Daddy's granny told us some very interesting stories about the old days. I learned more history from that old lady, in one afternoon, than I had in my entire lifetime of going to school. After we had eaten lunch and listened to stories, granny took us on a tour of her house. Granny took her time and it seemed like an eternity. The last room that she showed us was her bedroom. It was a very beautiful room. To my surprise, the walls were covered with pictures of me. Daddy looked surprised too. I asked granny about the girl in all of the pictures, the girl that looked exactly like me. Granny told us that these were pictures of her when she was a young girl. The ride back home was very quiet. We were both in deep thought. I kept thinking to myself, Daddy is my real father. His doctors told him that he was sterile. Doctors make mistakes just like everyone else. Nothing in this world is one hundred per cent. I had to know the truth. If there was a chance that Daddy was my real father, then I had to know. When we got home, I talked to mommy and Daddy about my theory. My theory was pretty well thought out. I came to the conclusion that when mommy broke up with my so-called father, Daddy consoled her. Daddy consoled her all night long. I was conceived that very night. Mommy and Daddy looked at each other and started laughing. They looked at me and saw that I was dead serious. There was silence for a couple of minutes. Mommy told me that she would talk to my so-called father about taking a DNA test. She told me not to get my hopes up. It took awhile but my so-called father agreed to get DNA tested. He must have thought about how good it would be if he did not have to pay child support.

A wise man once wrote that truth will set you free. I have never felt so free. The man who raised me, the man who loves my mommy and I with all of his heart, is my real father. Maybe my conception was a miracle, maybe it wasn't. All I know is I have my Daddy. God bless the child who has her own.

17. GREEN

There are many colors in a rainbow. The spectrum of colors range from dark to light. Without all of these colors the rainbow does not exist. Color is one of the ways that Man divides himself from other men. Man has always been a segregated creature. While all men were created equally, all men are not the same. If all men looked, acted, and thought alike, the world would be a very bland and boring place to live. It would be like having a world full of clones. That is why the Creator made so many beautiful shades of people and allowed these people to think for themselves. Although there are many ways to classify the many different varieties of men, color is the chosen method. In the brief history of man, every race has had the chance to rule. Every race has been unjust. Every color has failed.

In the year 2200 A.D., everyone wants to be an individual. Yet, everyone wants to fit in. There are no clear cut races and the only color that matters, is the color of your money. Green!!! The amount of money you had determined your status in life. If you had no Green, you were treated like a leper. Society's elite would have your face painted Green to show the world that you had no Green. Just like in previous societies, the few control the many. The few had most of the Green.

Elroy P. Moneybaggs had lots of Green. He lived large. He was at the top of the food chain. His appetite for Green was enormous. He got his hands on as much wealth as he could. It did not bother him to see friends and relatives, who had lost their Green, walking around with green painted faces of shame. He still had his Green and that's all that mattered to him.

At the beginning of the Great Revolution, Green was distributed equally among the people. Keep your Green and be somebody. Lose your Green and life would be Hell on Earth. That was the Law. One by one, people started losing their Green. Bad financial decisions, economic disasters, scams, health problems, etc.., all contributed to the loss of Green. Whatever the reason, Green was lost and the people were divided once more. You were not allowed to earn more Green. The only way to get more Green, was to get a relative to give or Will you some Green. The crime rate skyrocketed. Jails filled up at an alarming rate. Those with Green were the only people allowed to vote. They passed unfair laws that allowed them to make life time servants, slaves, out of those who had lost their Green. The faces of those people who had no Green were painted green. When you lose your Green, you lose all of your rights and you are treated like cattle or wild dogs. It's really amazing how Man keeps making the same mistakes over and over. History just keeps on repeating it's self.

Elroy P. Moneybaggs was a very confident individual. Having lots of Green makes you confident. Elroy thought that he would always have Green. The thought of losing his Green, never crossed Elroy's mind. He never saw it coming. Elroy had many servants. He treated them very badly. He did not have a lot of friends because he was an asshole. He climbed to the top of the social ladder, stepping on anyone who got in his way. The higher you climb up the social ladder, the harder the fall is to the bottom. Elroy loved fine wine and fine women. He spent lots of his Green on both. He bought his women expensive gifts like cars, houses and jewelry. His love for wine sent him on wild drinking binges. While drunk, he would gamble and lose large sums. Sometimes he would get robbed while staggering home from the nearest tavern. Since he did not have many friends, he paid people to hang out with him. Elroy was losing his keen sense for business and started making some bad business deals. The roof really caved in on Elroy when he got hurt. He was out riding his prized horse and fell off. Elroy was paralyzed from the waste down. Huge medical bills started to drain Elroy's Green. He sold the rights to over half of his servants to pay bills. He did not have enough servants to harvest his crops. The crops were rotting in the fields. Elroy lost all of his Green. The master became the slave.

Elroy was arrested for not paying his bills. Society ruled that Elroy had to have his face painted Green, the ultimate humiliation. The thought of having a green face filled Elroy with terror. On the day that Elroy was scheduled to have his face painted, a family member died and left Elroy lots of Green. It seems that fortune has a way of smiling on those that do not deserve it. Elroy was still a paralyzed man but that did not matter to him. He had his Green back and that's all that he cared about. He learned little or nothing from his ordeal. He became an even bigger asshole than he had been before he lost his Green.

Another Revolution has come and gone. You can't treat people badly and not expect them to react violently. With 90 per cent of the people walking around with green faces, a revolt was eminent. It happened quickly. What set it off? Nobody knows how or exactly when it started. In the dark of the night, the wealthy were overrun and taken away. They were never seen or heard from again. Green was once again distributed equally to all of the people. Laws were changed and having servants or slaves was illegal. All of the green paint was destroyed.

18. LOVE LETTER TO MY BOO

DEAR BOO,

During the many years that I have known you, you have helped me to be the kind of person that I have always wanted to be. Without you, I would never had been able to make a change in my life. I was blessed from the very first time that we met. You were an Angel sent from heaven at a time when I needed an Angel in my life. You have helped me stay strong. You have helped me stay focussed.

I am a very stubborn person and I have always resisted change. Once I got into a comfort zone, there was no changing me. In order for us to be together, to form a lasting union, I had to change. I had always taken care of myself. I liked being able to control the things around me. There was never any stress or drama, never any excitement. I was a loner and I enjoyed time to myself. At least I thought that I did. My behavior was set and I kept things in their proper place. Then it happened. Wham !! You came into my life and totally disrupted my program. You taught me how to care about someone else. You taught me how to share my life with someone else. You taught me about love. No longer did I only think about my own happiness. I fought the changes with all of my might and I am so glad that I lost that fight. Having someone that I could depend on and someone that depended on me was great. You were my best friend. I never ever thought that I could have a female friend. I felt that sooner or later, hormones would kick in and the friendship would be over. That never happened to us. When the time was right, we became lovers. You watched my back and I watched yours. When I was down and out, you helped pick me up. We were always together, two of a kind. When you felt pain, I felt pain. We were very careful not to crowd each other. We gave each other space. We gave each other respect. Thank you so much for being you. Lord knows that I made some real bad decisions while we were together, but you were never critical. We survived the bad times and enjoyed the good times.

Before I met you, I had a very cloudy view of romance. Quite frankly, I had no idea what romance was. Romance was just a game to me. You did what you had to to get in side of those panties. Loving somebody for a long time was not a part of the game. Now I know that real romance is an everyday thing. It's just like a newborn baby, keep on feeding it and it grows, stop feeding it and it dies. Our romance was and always will be fresh and alive.

The thought of being without you is an unbearable thought, indeed. Waking up to your wonderful smile, walking hand in hand, making love all night long, those are just a few of my favorite things. We are but mere mortals and we don't live forever. I had hoped that we would last forever. I know that our love will last forever even if we do not. Here I stand, overcome by my grief, filled with loneliness and pain, writing you this letter that you will never be able to read. I know that you are still with me in spirit and that gives me comfort. I am placing this letter inside of your golden casket. This is my final goodbye to you. I hope to see you again in heaven.

GOODBYE MY LOVE

19. FARMER IN THE DELL

Billy Ray was once a very successful farmer. He had lots of property and lots of money. He started off pretty poor. Billy Ray's father had been a life time farmer and so had his father and his father's father. Farming is something that Billy Ray wanted no parts of. Billy Ray had watched his father struggle with farming, year after year. His father worked extremely hard but usually he had little or nothing at the end of the farming season. Billy Ray never understood why his father would put so much time, effort, blood, and sweat into farming when it wasn't paying off. His father was a fourth generation farmer and farming was in his blood. Farming was in Billy Ray's blood too. He just didn't know it at the time. Billy Ray was determined that he was not going to be a poor country farmer like his father. When it came to Billy Ray's career choices, farming was definitely not one of them. Billy Ray was very ambitious. He wanted to become a doctor or a lawyer. Those were noble professions that made lots of money. Billy Ray gave higher education his best effort.

Unfortunately, Billy Ray was never good when it came to school work. He had barely graduated from high school. He did not have the grades to get into college. Billy Ray didn't have classroom smarts but he did have street smarts. Billy Ray had to swallow his pride and go to work on his father's farm.

Billy Ray's father died unexpectedly one summer. Billy Ray had to take over and run the family farm. Billy Ray's father died with a lot of debt. That debt was inherited by Billy Ray. Billy Ray turned out to be a pretty good business man, but he was a lousy farmer. He tried his luck at growing almost every crop that could be grown, including weed. If effort alone was a measure of success, then Billy Ray would have been very successful. With mounting debt and failing crops, things were looking pretty bleak. Billy Ray was seriously thinking about filing for bankruptcy protection. He put it off for as long as he could but he decided that bankruptcy was his only choice.

After a very restless night, Billy Ray got dressed and decided to drive into town and file for bankruptcy protection. He was just about to open the door to his car when the mailman pulled up. He got his mail and began looking it over. It was the usual stack of bills, junk

107

mail, and repossession letters. At the bottom of the stack of mail, there was a green envelope. Inside of the green envelope was a note and a first class ticket to Ireland. The note was addressed to Billy Ray. It gave him instructions to catch a plane to Ireland immediately and to wait to be picked up. The note stated that this was a once in a lifetime opportunity and that room and board would be provided free of charge. Billy Ray was tempted to throw the note and the first class plane ticket away. He did not know anyone that lived in Ireland. He thought that this was some kind of trick. After hours of deliberations, he made the decision to go for it. He packed a suitcase and drove to the airport. The flight to Ireland was very long. Flying first class made the trip a whole lot better. This was Billy Ray's first flight. He had the jitters at first but he soon calmed down. After the plane landed in Ireland, Billy Ray was the last passenger to get off. At the bottom of the off ramp, was a little man, a very little man. The little man greeted Billy Ray with a smile and a handshake. He told Billy Ray that he was very happy that Billy Ray had accepted his invitation. The little man introduced himself to Billy Ray. He said that he was called Lucky. Billy Ray started laughing and said, "Lucky Charm?" The little man said yes, that was indeed his name. Lucky traveled by horse and carriage. He took Billy Ray to his home, deep in the woods. Lucky's home was built inside of a very big tree. It was a very strange place for a person to live but it had all of the comforts of any modern home. There was a very grand meal on the dining room table. Lucky and Billy Ray ate until they couldn't eat anymore. They relaxed by the fireplace. Billy Ray started asking questions. Lucky told Billy Ray that they both needed to get some sleep and that all questions would be answered first thing in the morning. Billy Ray went into a deep sleep. Two weeks later, Billy Ray woke up.

Lucky was not an ordinary man. In fact, Lucky wasn't a man at all. Lucky was a leprechaun. Lucky had lived in Ireland for over two hundred years. He had accumulated an endless amount of wealth and power. The one thing that Lucky could not do, was to leave Ireland. Lucky yearned to see all of the places that he had seen on satellite television. Lucky wanted to experience other cultures. Lucky had finally found a spell that would allow him to leave Ireland. Lucky needed to transfer his spirit into a willing, compatible person. After years of searching, Lucky found a person who was compatible, Billy

Ray was the one. Lucky could not force Billy Ray to go along with his plan. He had to convince him to go along with his plan.

Billy awoke from his deep sleep. Lucky explained his plan to Billy Ray. Lucky made Billy Ray an offer, an offer that he could not refuse. In return for his services, Lucky was going to make Billy Ray the most successful farmer ever and one of the world's wealthiest men. Billy Ray, who had already hit rock bottom, agreed to the plan. At midnight, Lucky and Billy Ray went outside. Lucky recited a spell over and over. There was a flash of light and the transfer was made. Lucky vanished and his spirit entered the body of Billy Ray. On the way to the airport, Lucky told Billy Ray to go to the field at the end of the forest. In that field, a very special plant grew. This was the plant that Billy Ray was to grow on his farm. It looked just like a blue sweet potato. Billy Ray put the plant in his suitcase. Billy Ray bought a plane ticket and flew home. Lucky had put two million dollars in Billy Ray's bank account. Once home, Billy Ray paid off all of his debt and bought brand new farm equipment. Lucky wanted to travel the world so that is just what Lucky and Billy Ray did. They traveled around for about a year. They ended their travels back in Ireland.

Lucky transferred his spirit out of Billy Ray. Lucky instructed Billy Ray on how to grow the special plant that they had taken a year earlier. Lucky thanked Billy Ray, they said their goodbyes and parted company.

Billy Ray arrived home and got to work, planting his new plant. He named the new plant after his father, Daddy Blue Potato. He dug a six inch hole and placed the new plant inside of the hole, covered the roots of the new plant with first quality dirt and manure. He gave the plant plenty of water. Two minutes after it was planted, the new plant started growing and reproducing. Within a half hour, the fields were completely covered by this strange new plant. The very next day, Daddy Blue Potatoes were ready to be harvested. Billy Ray had been told by Lucky that this was a very special food. These potatoes, when eaten, tasted like any kind of food that the person eating them thought about. If you thought about pork chops, the potatoes tasted exactly like pork chops. The potatoes were very addictive too. Billy Ray sat in the middle of the field, eating potato after potato, until he felt too full to walk. It was if he had just eaten a gourmet meal fit for a king. This was a very special plant indeed.

Billy Ray took a truck load of his new food product to the local produce market. There, he set up a booth and began selling Daddy Blue Potatoes. He gave away samples while he explained what this new food product was. The people went wild over the Daddy Blue Potatoes. Billy Ray sold out in record time. After a couple of weeks of great sales, Billy Ray knew that the world was ready for his new food product. Word soon spread about this new food product. People were calling from all over the world, trying to order Daddy Blue Potatoes. Billy Ray had more business than one man could handle, so he hired a crew of pickers and a crew of office workers. Daddy Blue Potatoes only grew on Billy Ray's farm. Billy Ray hired security people and put up an electric fence around his entire farm. He was fast becoming one of the world's wealthiest farmers.

Billy Ray went from being a nobody and bankrupt to being wealthy and famous. Success brings a lot of good things with it, but it also brings some pretty bad things with it too. Governments, businesses, wealthy people, all wanted a piece of the action. Billy Ray was threatened, sued, and robbed quite often, but he still managed to stay ahead of the game. Billy Ray was very successful but he was getting tired of the rat race.

It had been thirty years since Billy Ray had received the green envelope from Lucky. Billy Ray had completely forgotten about his pint sized benefactor. On this day, Billy Ray received another green envelope from Lucky. A letter in the envelope stated that Lucky was dying and that he wanted to see Billy Ray one last time. Billy Ray flew to Ireland right away. To Billy Ray's surprise, the little leprechaun was not at the airport to greet him. Billy Ray rented a vehicle and drove to Lucky's home. Lucky's giant tree house was burned to the ground. Lucky was not around. Billy Ray called out Lucky's name. A lightning bolt struck the spot where Lucky's tree house once stood. Lucky appeared out of the ashes. Lucky and Billy Ray shook hands and sat down on a log. Lucky asked Billy Ray about all of his experiences since the last time that they saw each other. Billy Ray told Lucky everything. He told Lucky that he was growing weary of the whole business world. Lucky was glad to hear that Billy Ray was growing weary. He told Billy Ray that it was time for him to leave this mortal world. Lucky had sent for Billy Ray so that Billy

Ray could replace him. Billy Ray agreed to replace Lucky as a helping leprechaun. Billy Ray left his business to his family members and never left Ireland again. Daddy's Blue Potatoes never grew again. When Billy Ray came to Ireland, the potatoes on his farm dissappeared.

20. STOP SIGN

I sit outside of my door each day. I watch the intersection. I watch the Stop Sign. With my trusty rifle by my side, I keep watch. The local people know why I do what I do. They remember the tragedy. They remember the funerals. They know the rules of the Stop Sign. They know that if they brake the rules, they will be fired upon. I have blown out many a tire since I started my watching.

It began a year ago. On a clear, hot morning, I witnessed the tragedy. I can remember it like it happened yesterday. When I woke up that morning, a very bad feeling came over me. I knew that something bad was about to happen. I just did not know exactly what was going to happen. If I knew, maybe I could have done something to change things. I usually take my dog Smitty for early morning walks. I called out to Smitty but he did not want to go outside. I think that Smitty had the same bad feeling. I chased him around the house. I caught him and put his leash on him. It was a very beautiful day. With each step that I took, the bad feeling grew stronger and stronger.

115

Smitty was acting scared and nervous. He kept on looking back and forth. He was having a hard time breathing too.

I use to drive. It has been a very long time since I last drove. The thing that I hated most about driving, was coming to an intersection and stopping at a stop sign. There is always one or two idiots who don't understand the rules of the Stop Sign. There should be a special driving class to teach people what to do at a Stop Sign. The rule is plenty simple. If you stop first you go first. Somehow, drivers have gotten the idea that you are suppose to stop and play peek-a-boo. Drivers make a simple rule very complex. There is your over courteous driver, who confuses everybody else by waving them on, letting everybody go ahead no matter what order they stop. This does not help anybody. All it does is breaks the rule, stop first, go first. There are also drivers that think that they should go first. These types of drivers don't care who stops first. These are very ignorant drivers. The most dangerous drivers of all, are those drivers that do not stop at all. When I drove, I always obeyed the rule. If I stopped first, I went first. The stupidity of some drivers simply amazes me. I stopped driving because of a Stop Sign. A drunk driver ran a Stop Sign. That driver plowed into my vehicle, injuring me and killing my wife and kids. That drunk bastard died too. If he had not died, I would have killed him my self.

On that very bad day, when Smitty and I went walking, four very different people were on their way to four different destinations. They did not know that they would end up at the same exact spot. Smitty and I arrived at the crosswalk at the intersection of Congress Avenue and Dixie Court. We were reluctant to cross the street because four vehicles were coming. The four vehicles arrived at the intersection at the same time. Inside of an old Chevy Nova, was Carla, a college student on her way to class. Inside the Volvo, was Mrs. Dean, a retired teacher on her way to the grocery store. Driving the Mercedes, was Winston, a stock broker on his way to his downtown office. Lex, driving the Ford truck, was on his way to work at a nearby construction site. They all waited at their Stop Sign. For a long twenty seconds, nobody would go through the intersection. It seemed like an eternity. Each person waited on the other to proceed. Who goes first when everybody stopped at the same time. Tension was building as each driver waved to the others to go on through. When nobody moved, everybody started blowing their horns. A line of traffic was forming behind each vehicle. I looked at Smitty and Smitty looked at me. We knew this was it, the event that we had dreaded all morning long. Motors roared as each driver floored their gas pedals. A deafening crash was followed by explosions and by fire. Death came instantly to each driver.

I buried Smitty that evening. Smitty was a casualty of the Stop Sign too. The stress proved too much for Smitty's old little heart to handle. Two major Stop Sign tragedies have changed me forever. I don't drive any more. I don't go for walks any more. I lost my wife and kids, along with my best friend, Smitty. Four other people lost their lives too. All because of a Stop Sign. If you stop first, you go first. What is so hard about that? The City is replacing the Stop Sign with a traffic light. Until they do replace the Stop Sign, I will be here on guard. I will be here with my rifle, waiting. I will make sure that the drivers obey the rules of the Stop Sign.

21. FIEND

A few very short months ago, a friend of mine, the editor of a major magazine, commissioned me to write an essay about drug abuse. I am the right person for the job because I have been a drug abuse counselor for the last ten years. I guess you could say that I am pretty much an expert on the subject of drug abuse. It took me a little time to get started. There were so many possibilities, so many topics to write about. I decided to write about one of my clients who had died a horrible death related to drug abuse.

There are a lot of people who know someone or who know about someone who has abused drugs. Some people can kick their habit and some people can't. The people that can't kick their habit, usually become fiends. A fiend can be described as a demon, a devil, a malicious foe. Another description for a fiend is someone who is crazy about something. My patient, Dwayne Smith, was most definitely a fiend. Dwayne Smith was crazy about something. He was crazy about drugs and the high that they gave him. He would do almost anything to get his hands on some drugs. He would lie, cheat, steal, whatever it took. Some of his drugs of choice included LSD, crack, cocaine, morphine, heroin, and weed. In my ten years of drug counseling, I have seen them come and I have seen them go. I have worked with doctors, lawyers, mayors, school teachers, and librarians. Nobody is immune to drug addiction. Dwayne Smith was certainly not.

Dwayne Smith was raised by his aunt. His parents died in a plane crash when Dwayne was just a baby. His aunt did all she could to raise Dwayne to be a good person. She spoiled him, in my opinion. Dwayne had all of the benefits that a middle class life could bring. Dwayne was an extremely intelligent young man. In high school, he was class president and valedictorian. He was also captain of the baseball, football, and basketball teams. Dwayne was a natural born leader. He accepted an academic scholarship to one of the nation's best colleges. College is where Dwayne's addiction got started.

During Dwayne's freshman year at college, things were going quite well. Dwayne's roommate was a senior who liked to drink. His roommate kept a keg of refrigerated beer in their room. Dwayne did not drink or smoke. He didn't even take aspirin. Towards the end of the school year, after trying all year to get Dwayne to try some beer, Dwayne's roommate convinced him to try a glass of ice cold beer. Dwayne discovered that he liked beer. The next school year, Dwayne moved off campus into his very own apartment. He got his own keg of refrigerated beer. Midway through the year, Dwayne went from beer drinker to pot smoker. For awhile, that is as far as Dwayne would go. He left the hard drugs alone. Then Dwayne met Elsa. He met her at a little upscale club on the ritzy side of town. Elsa was sensational. She was a super fine goddess. She was also into coke, and I don't mean Coca Cola. After dating for a short time, Dwayne fell deeply in love with Elsa. Elsa told Dwayne that they could not be a couple until they did everything together. She convinced Dwayne to try cocaine. He tried it and he became addicted. During the next two years, Dwayne's grades took a downward flight. He lost his academic scholarship and was eventually kicked out of school. Dwayne's romance with Elsa ended when his money ran out and he could no longer support two drug addicts.

Dwayne moved back home with his aunt. He did not tell her that he was kicked out of school. He told her that he was burnt out and that he needed a break from school work. Dwayne needed to be high daily so he started stealing from his aunt. At first he would steal little things, things that his aunt would not readily miss. As his addiction grew, his boldness grew. Dwayne would spend hours in his locked room snorting cocaine. Things, like the television, dissappeared from the house. Dwayne's aunt would ask him about the missing items and he would slick talk her. When she would ask about the television, Dwayne would tell her that he traded it in for a better television that should be arriving any day now. The better television never came. After three more televisions and two VCR's disappear, Dwayne's aunt caught on. She loved him dearly but she, being a nurse, understood that Dwayne had a serious problem. She knew that if she didn't act fast, Dwayne was going to steal her blind. That is when Dwayne and I first met. His aunt enrolled him in a rehabilitation clinic where I was working. I didn't get to work with Dwayne at that time because he snuck out the back door of the clinic.

Dwayne Smith went on a crime spree to support his addiction. He lived in and out of homeless shelters. He was snatching purses, car jacking, and breaking into homes. Dwayne Smith was the reason that every house in the city had alarm systems. Dwayne was a fiend but he was still a genius. He figured out how to get around or how to disable the alarm systems. Someone said that a mind is a terrible thing to waste. Dwayne Smith is proof of that. He became friends with everybody's watch dog, bringing them steaks and doggie treats. He was like a criminal Santa Claus, sliding down chimneys. Eventually he was caught. He was put in drug rehabilitation. That is when I met Dwayne for the second time. That is when I was able to find out some things about him and try to help him.

Dwayne Smith's best friends were drugs. They talked to him each day. Drugs gave Dwayne confidence and respect. Once drugs were in his bloodstream, they made everything better. They taught him. They counseled him. They made love to him. Drugs showed Dwayne how to put his intelligence to proper use. Several months passed. I thought that Dwayne and I were making progress. That's when Dwayne suffered a relapse. Once again, Dwayne ran off and dissappeared.

Dwayne got a job in a nursing home. While working at the nursing home, he would steal medications meant for patients. He was eventually caught stealing and was sent back to the rehabilitation clinic. He was kept locked up in a very secure, padded room. Therapy was long and hard. It had to be. Dwayne was a very good actor. He fooled my staff and I into thinking that we were making some real progress. After a year and a half, Dwayne was put on probation and allowed to leave the clinic. For awhile, Dwayne was a model citizen. He went back to school and got himself a part time job. He reported to his probation officer on a daily basis. Then one day, Dwayne disappeared. He failed to report in to his probation officer. There was a warrant issued for his arrest. His aunt called us to tell us that she had received a post card from Dwayne. The post card came from Haiti. Dwayne had pulled off a series of bank robberies and bolted to Haiti.

Dwayne stayed high in Haiti. He lived the good life until his stolen money ran out. It seems that his luck ran out too. Dwayne stole drugs from a Haitian Witch Doctor. The Witch Doctor put a spell on Dwayne which made him very sick. Dwayne wrote to his Aunt. He asked her to send him a ticket home. When Dwayne's plane landed from Haiti, his Aunt, the police, and I were waiting for him. When Dwayne saw us he wanted to run but he was too weak. He was taken to the hospital where test were done. Physically, Dwayne was okay. For a junky, he was in real good health. When Dwayne went to sleep, he never woke back up. Cause of death was unknown. Dwayne's Aunt had his body cremated. When she went to pick up the ashes, there were no ashes. Turns out that the Haitian Witch Doctor paid some men to steal Dwayne's ashes and to bring the ashes back to Haiti. The Witch Doctor mixed Dwayne's ashes with some Haitian herbs and made a powerful drug. The Haitian people swear that one dose will keep you high for a year. It even cures the common cold.

22. LITTLE GIRL LOST

Once upon a time, there lived a little orphan girl. She was lost and alone in a very big world. Most of her time was spent searching for love and acceptance. She was moved from foster home to foster home but never did she find a loving home. She grew up and became a very beautiful woman. During her search for love, she became pregnant. The father of her unborn child moved away after she told him that she was pregnant. Alone, feeling unloved, she vowed to give her child the love and the affection that she never received. A baby girl was born. Her name was Nicole.

Nicole and her mother were inseparable. Nicole loved her mother with all of her heart. Nicole never missed having a father because her mother treated her so well. For the first seven years of her life, Nicole was spoiled rotten. It was just her and her mother. They were very happy in their private little world. Then it happened, her mother found true love. Her mother started dating a man that she had met at work. Nicole felt that she was being left out. She was seeing less and less of her mother each week. Nicole was often left in the care of a babysitter while her mother was being romanced, swept off of her feet. Nicole felt like she was being abandoned. Nicole felt like she was losing her mother, the love of her life. This was the same mother that told her over and over again, that she loved her and her only, that she would never leave her, that she would never let anyone or anything separate them. Nicole talked less and less until she stopped talking to anyone. Nicole's mother took her to see many doctors to find out why she stopped talking. They could not give her an answer.

Nicole's mother got married in a private ceremony. Nicole and her mother moved in with her stepfather. He was a wealthy man with a big house. He seemed to be a very nice man but Nicole hated him. The more that he tried to treat Nicole like a daughter, the more she hated him. He had come between Nicole and her mother and she despised him for that. Nicole's mother and father tried to have a loving and happy home but Nicole's hatred and unhappiness was putting a strain on their relationship. The stepfather knew that Nicole hated him and he didn't know why. He had tried everything that he knew to win her over. He eventually turned to drinking. One day he

127

had a little too much to drink. He was drunk as a skunk. He got loud and became violent. He hit Nicole's mother. Nicole reached into a closet, found a golf club, and went to work on her stepfather. He was left partially crippled from Nicole's attack. Although she was only eight at the time, she was a lot stronger than she looked. Nicole's mother took the side of her husband and had Nicole committed to a mental hospital for observation. Nicole didn't blame her mother, whom she loved unconditionally, she blamed her stepfather. Nicole wanted him gone. Something had to be done to get rid of this man who had intruded into their happy little world. While in the mental hospital, Nicole started making plans, plotting her strategy. After a couple of months, she was allowed home on the weekends. She pretended to be happy. She acted well, like everything was fine, like a nice little girl. Eventually, Nicole was allowed to come home. A couple of weeks after Nicole was allowed home, her stepfather's dead body was found laying at the bottom of the stairwell. He had a broken neck from his fall.

After the funeral, Nicole and her mother moved to a smaller house. Once again, it was just the two of them, Nicole and her mother.

They were close again. Nicole was talking more and more each day. Then it happened again. Her mother fell in love with a nice gentleman and got married for a second time. Nicole knew exactly what had to be done. This time her new stepfather was found dead in the family pool. Apparently he was electrocuted when a radio fell into the pool. To Nicole, he was just another intruder. He had stolen her mother's love and he was dealt with. One accidental death could be explained away, but two accidental deaths in less than a year raised a few eyebrows. Nicole and her mother moved thousands of mile away to the east coast. There they would get a fresh start.

Husband number three didn't fare much better. He was mauled to death by the family dog. Nicole had trained the dog for months to hate stepfather number three. Nicole's mother didn't want to believe that her daughter, her little angel, had anything to do with the deaths of her husbands. She tried to rationalize each situation but the evidence kept pointing to Nicole. Finally, Nicole's mother asked her point blank about the deaths of her husbands. Nicole had no problem telling her mother that she had killed each of her stepfathers. She told her mother that if she got married again, she would kill that stepfather too.

Nicole's mother couldn't believe what she had just heard. Her deepest fears were confirmed. Nicole's mother picked up the telephone to call the police and turn her daughter in. Nicole snatched the telephone out of her mother's hand and cracked her mother in the head with the telephone. Her mother was knocked out cold. Nicole dragged her mother down into the basement.

Fifteen years later, police were called by a neighbor. A rotting smell was coming from within the house that Nicole and her mother called home. The police broke down the front door. The smell of death knocked them to their knees. They had to go back outside and get respirators from their police car. The police entered the house for the second time. They found that the horrible rancid smell was coming from the basement. The police went down the stairs that led to the basement. There they were, Nicole and her mother. They had been dead for quite a while. It looked like a murder-suicide had taken place. Nicole had used a rope to tie her mother's dead body up in a sitting position in a chair. Nicole took some poison, sat in her mother's lap, and wrapped her arms around her mother. There they stayed until the police found them. The police tried to figure out what had happened. Nicole and her mother kept to themselves. Their neighbors could not give the police any clues. The deaths were ruled murder and suicide.

In this world that we live in, everybody needs and wants love. Nicole and her mother needed and wanted love. They did not understand the true power of love. Love is a very powerful force that can either make you very happy or make you very dead.

23. WORKING WITH DEATH

The ad said, "Help wanted, a real killer job, the last job that you will ever have ". My father always told me that if something sounds too good to be true, it's bad. I was broke, on my last leg. I had applied all over town for work. I already responded to every ad in the paper. This was a new ad, so I went for it. The ad stated that you had to apply in person. I copied the address from the ad and I hitchhiked to the location of the interview site. It was a very familiar location. I had been past this site a thousand times and I don't remember this office building being here. The office building appeared to be brand spanking new. It was also empty. I went inside to the front desk. There was a service bell. I rang the bell. I waited a few minutes. Nobody answered the bell. I had an uneasy feeling in my gut so I started to leave. When I got to the door, the elevator door at the end of the hallway opened up. My good sense told me to leave. Being broke and hungry, I was in no condition to listen to my good sense. I got into the elevator. There were no buttons to push, no floor levels. The elevator door closed and the elevator started moving downward. Faster and faster it went until it slowed down and it came to a smooth stop. The elevator door opened to what appeared to be a banquet. There was food everywhere. I did not hesitate to help my self to some of the food. I ate till I passed out. When I woke up, I was in a very chic office. I was sitting at a very large desk. Across from me, sitting in a throne type chair, was a very elderly gentleman. He asked if I ate and slept well. I told him that I ate like a pig and slept like a log. He told me that his company liked to be very very hospitable to hopeful employees. He introduced himself as John Doe, Human Resources Director.

The interview was very unusual. I asked John Doe exactly what would I be doing. John Doe told me that I would be working with Death, killing people. I went along with the gag, figuring that I was being tested. I asked John Doe what else I had to do. He told me that was all that I would be doing. He told me that I would be killing good people as well as bad people, young people as well as old people. I would be working with Death who was contracted out to the devil, and sometimes contracted out by the Creator. This gag was ceasing to be funny to me. I told John Doe that I came to interview for a job, not to be played with. Sternly, John Doe told me that this was no game, to even interview for this position, you have to be already dead yourself. A chill ran down my spine. I told John Doe that I should not be interviewing if that is the case because I am very much alive. John Doe took out a gun and shot me in the head. The bullet passed through me and made a big hole in the wall. I was dead alright. I asked John Doe how long had I been dead and how did I die. According to John Doe, I died of a heart attack at a banquet, over three years ago.

I got the job on a trial basis. If Death liked working with me, the job was mine until our services were no longer needed. I expected Death to look like the images that I had always seen, skull, dark cape, glowing eyes, long pole with a curved blade attached. That was not how Death looked. Death looked like whatever he wanted to look like, whatever he needed to look like to get the job done. Death went from looking like an innocent high school kid to looking like a vicious animal.

My first assignments with Death really tested me. How I made it through them, I'll never know. The first killings were very personal to me. Death felt that if I got through those assignments, then the job was mine. The first outing with Death hit very close to home. We traveled to a Nursing Home. This was the same Nursing Home where my grandmother lived. I got a very bad feeling as we walked down a lonely hallway. My deepest fear came true as Death opened the door to my grandmother's room. I asked Death if he wanted me to kill my own grandmother. Death told me that I was just along for the experience and that I should watch and learn something. I thought that Death would be kind to grandmother and take her while she slept. That was not the case at all. Death waited until grandmother had to use the restroom to kill her. He gave her a stroke while she sat there on the toilet. I was angry with Death but I kept my cool. Later that day, we followed a minivan. Inside of the minivan was a mother and her newborn baby. I thought to my self, that lady just had a baby and Death is going to kill her. Turns out that it wasn't the mother that Death was after. The mother was just a fringe benefit. It was the newborn baby that Death had his sights on. I found my self riding in a semi-truck with Death. We plowed into the minivan, crushing the mother and her newborn baby. There were a lot more killings that day. Death and I were very active all over the world. I got the job.

Turns out that the current version of Death, was being forced to retire. I was being groomed as his successor. I was more than ready to take over. I had new and innovative ideas. I came up with the mass killings, the suicide bombings, deadly riots, Ebola and other super viruses, etc... I was taking out whole villages and cities. The powers that be thought that I was being reckless. They thought that I was killing too many people whose time had not come. Eventually I was replaced and the old Death got his job back. Looks like I'm out of a job again.

THE END

ABOUT THE AUTHOR

Mark D. Bradley is from a suburb just north of Cincinnati, Ohio. He has written thousands of unpublished works. Among his works are poems, songs, plays and novels. Born to humble beginnings, he was the first in his family to graduate from college. He has worked in the professions of video making, music, photography, and teaching. Mark is very well traveled and very much into the world's many different cultures. Mark is single and has no children. Using his life experience and a very vivid imagination, he writes stories that you don't mind reading over and over again. His work is very understandable and very reader friendly.

www.ingramcontent.com/pod-product-compliance
Lightning Source LLC
Chambersburg PA
CBHW051411280526
45785CB00003B/1027

* 9 7 8 1 4 0 3 3 3 6 5 6 9 *